THE MAGIC POWER OF

COMMAND SELLING

How to Take Charge
of the Sale

THE MAGIC POWER OF

COMMAND SELLING

How to Take Charge

of the Sale

N. C. Christensen

PARKER PUBLISHING COMPANY, INC.

West Nyack, N.Y.

Library of Congress Cataloging in Publication Data

Christensen, N   C
   The magic power of command selling.

   1. Salesmen and salesmanship. I. Title.
HF5438.C544134   658.85   72-8012
ISBN 0-13-545269-4

Other Books by the Author:

The Art of Persuasion in Selling
The Art of Persuasion for Sales Managers

HOW THE MAGIC OF COMMAND SELLING CAN TAKE CHARGE FOR YOU

This book presents to you the keys which can open doors to greater success, to higher financial rewards for you through the magic power of Command Salesmanship.

This book reveals clearly how you can profit by applying the simple principles of Command, take-charge Selling. These tested principles work! They produce sales!

The basic doctrine of Command Selling, as outlined in this book, is *bold salesmanship*. This doctrine is stimulating. It inspires you to reach out for the riches which can be yours. For instance, the principle of "grin and bear it" can lift you up to greater heights in sales. This Command principle is presented for you to profit by on Page 145, in Chapter 9. In addition, the magic power of getting keyed up to sell more can give you a fresh view of your widening opportunities in the market place. This technique is explained on Page 114, in Chapter 7.

This how-to-do-it book has been written by a work-a-day salesman. It has been stripped of "gobbledegook" and of wild, untried theories. The principles of Command Selling come to you pre-tested. They are wholly practical, workable and profitable. The primary purpose of this book is to show you how you can rise above yourself and zoom your personal income to undreamed of heights. Its source is case records and personal experiences which reveal to you how you can enjoy spectacular rewards from take-charge selling. For instance, you will be introduced to five simple steps which are surefire attention getters. These steps are presented in the language of working salesmen on Page 66, in Chapter 4.

This book can vitalize your self-confidence and show you how to develop a bold sureness in your selling methods. You will be shown how to become a trusted sales consultant for your customers and your prospective customers through the principles of take-charge salesmanship as outlined in this unique book. This broader field in selling is presented on Page 170, in Chapter 11.

In this book you may find solutions to many problems which have kept your volume down. By applying the command principles presented you can turn sales slumps into sales volume. You will learn how other command salesmen have built greater and more profitable sales volume by applying the same principles presented here. This book presents a fresh concept of spectacular selling. On Page 53, in Chapter 3, you are shown how you can sell more by significant showmanship in your sales presentations. From the success experiences of others you can gain an insight into how you can turn command showmanship into sales volume and thereby enjoy greater income.

This book is packed with the combined experiences of men and women who have reaped the rewards of take-charge selling. It is a volume of tested principles for command performance in selling. It can take charge for you in the most exciting of all fields of commercial endeavor—selling.

N. C. C.

CONTENTS

THE MAGIC POWER OF

COMMAND SELLING

How to Take Charge
of the Sale

CHAPTER ONE

HOW TO DEVELOP COMMAND SELLING PROSPECTING TECHNIQUES

Salesmen who are breaking volume records in today's challenging market are demonstrating that the secret of success in selling is persistent, thorough prospecting.

Prospecting is simply the intelligent search for people who are qualified to become your customers. We might say that every person with visible means of support is a possible prospect. By skillful screening you can sift out the qualified prospects and concentrate your take-charge selling power on them. Take-charge salesmen succeed by take-charge prospecting. They perfect techniques which will assist them in building files of "live" prospects. Take-charge prospecting requires an insight into all areas which affect the market place. Consider, for example, the following five areas and what is required for success in take-charge selling:

1. *KNOWLEDGE* of your market.
2. *KNOWLEDGE* of "live" prospects.
3. *KNOWLEDGE* of other people who buy and who may buy from you.

4. *KNOWLEDGE OF WHAT MOTIVATES PEOPLE TO BUY.*

5. *KNOWLEDGE* of yourself and of your qualifications to take charge of any selling situation.

Arthur H. Clough, the British author, who was often gloomy in his outlook, did, however, pen this spur to action from which some take-charge sales people profit: "Grace is given by God, but *knowledge is bought in the market place.*"

The market place is a realistic place. There we learn the ways of people who buy and sell. As Samuel Johnson said: "Knowledge is of two kinds. We know a subject ourselves or we know where to find information about it."

One high-level salesman in the insurance field kept an interesting file. He packed it with knowledge about people, because people provided him with luxuries as well as with bread and butter. He packed into his prospect file clippings from newspapers and magazines. These clippings informed him of what someone had done or proposed to do. To these clippings he added his own personal notes. These notes shed additional light on those people. They became "live" prospects by this technique of take-charge prospecting. He dipped into this file often to get vital information about the hopes, the plans, the capacities of people. Thus he created sales out of bits of information. He had laid the ground work for persuasive selling by thorough, helpful, enlightening take-charge prospecting.

In another file this take-charge salesman kept data up to date about market developments. He made his territory a subject of deep study. He constantly searched for information about people who might buy. Then he qualified these people as a prerequisite to a well planned sales effort. He also searched for knowledge about his territory. He learned of its productive capacity. He found out how well the people in that market area prospered. In this way he gained an insight into supply and failure to supply the needs and wants of people in his territory. All of this fell into place for this take-charge salesman when he planned his calls. It protected him from going into the market place blindfolded. This knowledge armed him to take charge of selling situations. All this he achieved by the simple process of developing a method of thorough take-charge prospecting.

Eric A. Johnston, once called the "czar of the motion picture industry," due to his take-charge attitude as president of the Motion

Picture Association of America, was, in fact, a take-charge salesman. His business successes made it apparent that he had done his prospecting well. He constantly preached the doctrine of free enterprise which, in reality, is what success in take-charge selling is all about.

Take a look at the market today. It's constantly changing. Salesmen need more and more knowledge, and the fun of acquiring knowledge increases as we dig for information. Here are some facts that can come to you when you dig deeply in your take-charge prospecting:

Not long ago someone suggested that the market is in danger of saturation. Someone else went after this to get at the facts. One survey indicated that more than 40 percent of American families still do not own their homes. This leaves the real estate market open for a lot of hard selling. Another in-depth survey indicated that more than one-fifth of the families in this country do not own an automobile. Difficult to believe when you get tied up in a traffic jam on the freeway. But it does tell us that there is still a wide market for cars. And still another survey revealed that more than 21 percent of families had no life insurance. Would you call this market saturation?

The foregoing fields and many others provide opportunities for take-charge salesmen to enjoy riches in abundance. And, the foundation for that sort of sales success can be built with sound take-charge prospecting techniques. Let us now consider some of these techniques:

HOW TO FIND OUT WHAT YOU NEED TO KNOW ABOUT PROSPECTS FOR SUCCESS IN COMMAND SELLING

As a take-charge salesman, self-interest dictates that you know enough about your prospects to serve them well. You can learn about them without "snooping." You can learn about them by expanding communication, by showing sincere interest in them. Search for information that will build for you a service file, not a gossip file. Be knowledgeable about your prospects. It pays. Know about their needs, their wants, their aspirations, their interests, their hobbies, their way of life. You can gain much of this sort of knowledge of your prospects and put it to profitable use as a take-charge salesman. Will Rogers had a formula for living which few prospects or salesmen follow. It has a point in take-charge selling. The great humorist said: "Live your life so you wouldn't be afraid to sell the family parrot to the town gossip."

Here are three vital questions you need to have answered for take-charge selling:

1. *HOW DO THEY EARN THEIR LIVING?*
2. *WHAT ARE THEIR LIKES, THEIR DISLIKES, THEIR OBJECTIVES AND THEIR SPECIAL INTERESTS?*
3. *HOW CAN THEY BENEFIT BY BUYING WHAT YOU HAVE TO SELL?*

Here are four ways in which you can secure pertinent information about your prospects:

1. By listening.
2. By observing.
3. By inquiring.
4. By reading.

But, knowing is not enough, said Goethe. We must do. So it is in selling. We must act on the knowledge we gain about prospects —act persuasively. They must become convinced that it will profit them to become buyers. Only in that way does knowledge of prospects pay off for us.

Join the good listeners. They absorb much valuable information. They hear about people wherever they go—in coffee shops, at the bars, in the cloak rooms, in committee meetings, in air terminals, in bus stations, even at church. They develop the habit of listening attentively. Listening is an art, just as clear thinking is an art . . . and, as persuasion in selling is an art.

Likewise, look around you and develop the art of seeing. Keen observation may reveal much to you about your prospects. The ancients saw the wisdom in this, according to the 115th Psalm, in which we have this: "Eyes have they, but they see not." Vision is an asset for every take-charge salesman.

Tactful inquiry can open rich sources of information for take-charge salesmen. For instance, you may have read of an honor that has come to a prospect. Mention this to him. Ask him about the details. This will please him and he probably will open up and tell you more than you anticipated. To find out what you need to know ask of those who are in the best position to know.

Your newspapers, daily and weekly, may be rich sources of information about those to whom you expect to sell. Become an avid reader of both news and advertising. If a prospect's name appears favorably in print, clip it. At an opportune time tell him that you noticed his name in print. Such clippings should be filed. They often become profitable for take-charge salesmen.

Learn about the nature of a man's business by research into that particular business. The knowledge you gain will place you on favorable speaking terms with that prospect. This places you in a favorable position to take charge of a selling situation. By exchanging ideas with a prospect you establish communication which opens possibilities for profitable take-charge selling.

To the following suggested sources of information for what you need to know about prospects for success in take-charge selling add your own suggested sources:

THE "GAB" FEST—Man-to-man conversation yields much information.

THE PROSPECT'S ADVERTISING—This may reveal his point of view on business policy. Observe! See! Evaluate!

THE OCCASIONAL CALL—Visit a prospect's place of business to observe the class of patronage he caters to. Get a first-hand view of the operation.

KNOW THE CREDIT MANAGER—Ask him about a prospect. He may have a file loaded with pertinent information.

NEWSPAPER FILES—Back numbers of your local newspaper are usually available in the newspaper's library or in the public library. In them you can often find the names of prospects. Items may reveal club connections or other connections that a take-charge salesman can use to his advantage.

TELEPHONE DIRECTORIES—Classified sections often disclose the varied activities of a prospect.

SERVICE STATIONS—The attendant who cares for your prospect's car may fill you in on some things you'd like to know about your prospect if you establish friendly relations with that attendant.

WAITRESSES—The waitress in your prospect's favorite coffee shop may know what sort of guy your prospect is. She may even tell you about his personality if you are on speaking terms with her.

THE GARDENER—The man who keeps your prospect's lawn and shrubs in shape, or who keeps his church or his club surroundings beautiful may have a fresh slant on the man you hope to be able to sell your products to. What he knows may be yours if you establish communication with him.

THE PROSPECT FILE—Your own prospect cards, if well kept up, can become a productive source of ready-reference information. This requires research, note-making, listening, observing, inquiring and reading. These are pleasant tasks. Get "hooked" by the note book habit. It yields high dividends for take-charge salesmen.

HOW TO QUALIFY YOUR PROSPECTS AS TO THEIR NEEDS, THEIR WANTS AND THEIR ABILITY TO PAY FOR WHAT THEY BUY

Your prospects can be classified as *"LIVE," "PROMISING,"* or *"DOUBTFUL"* by finding out what you need to know about them.

"LIVE" PROSPECTS ARE READY FOR THE HARVEST OF THE TAKE-CHARGE SALESMAN.

"PROMISING" PROSPECTS challenge the take-charge salesman to go into action.

"DOUBTFUL" PROSPECTS dare the take-charge salesman to be bold, creative, imaginative, to be constructively helpful.

Take-charge sales people seldom drop any prospect as "impossible to be sold." The idea of dropping a prospect is foreign to take-charge salesmanship. Take-charge salesmen seek ways to turn doubtful prospects into buyers, but they rarely rate them as "impossible."

You may hear about prospects from their friendly associates, from their competitors, from those whom they patronize and from other acquaintances. Keep your eyes open for clues as to how your prospects operate. Strengthen communication lines between you and your prospects until you learn more and more about them. Suggest ways in which they can make more money by using the products or services which you sell. Their response to your suggestions may reveal much to you about their needs, their wants, their objectives and how they propose to reach those objectives. This knowledge gives you take-charge strength for increasing sales volume.

The technique of take-charge selling will draw you close to your prospects by convincing them that you have something which they need to attain their goals. By closing the communication gap between you and your prospect you place yourself in a position to take charge of the selling situation.

For instance, one of your prospects may be a merchant who should be buying goods from you for resale. He will buy your goods for only one purpose—to make money. The take-charge salesman hammers away on that self-interest. Over and over again he strives to show that prospect that he can make money by reselling the products he has for sale. When you can prove to your prospect by presenting convincing facts that what you have for sale has brought profits to others, that prospect begins to yield. This is take-charge selling which adds volume to your sales record.

Let us assume that you are a specialty salesman and that you have done your homework well. You have qualified your list of "live" and "promising" prospects. On your first call you rely heavily on observation to guide you in the right approach to convince your prospect that he will benefit by buying from you. Soon you become aware of how favorably you have impressed him. As you show him how others have profited by using your product or service your prospect's response may tip you off that he, too, has done considerable planning. He wonders whether what you have to sell will fit into his plans. At that point, by being well-informed about your product and about your prospect, take-charge salesmanship can have its finest hour.

HOW TO CONVERT KNOWLEDGE OF PROSPECTS INTO SALES

Knowledge of prospective customers, as well as knowledge of customers we already have in the bag, is an asset which none of us who work in the brief-case and sample-case league should take lightly. Yet, some of us do. One man in the top production bracket who had repeatedly startled his colleagues by topping their sales records, makes this point:

"Knowledge of prospects and of customers is of little real value to the salesman until he converts that knowledge into sales."

This same take-charge salesman prodded a large sales group representing many lines by this statement:

> Until I learned one simple principle, and understood it well, I made little progress in developing sales in volume, even among my so-called "steady customers." To develop sales volume with established customers I had to learn that mere order taking was not enough. I had to learn that steady customers were just as vulnerable to creative, imaginative selling as were the new prospects on whom I had been exerting much greater selling effort.

I also had to learn that no customer is, in fact, a "steady customer." Steady customers are the products of take-charge salesmanship in action in every call made on them.

Here, then, are four ways to convert your knowledge of prospects into sales:

1. *USE THE SALES POWER* of endorsements of users of your products.
2. *USE THE SALES POWER* of verified, indisputable case records which show benefits derived from the use of what you have to sell.
3. *USE THE SALES POWER* of your own experience and observation in marketing and selling.
4. *USE THE SALES POWER* of referring your prospective buyer to someone whom he knows and who you know has profited by using what you have to sell.

The overall principle which governs the effectiveness of take-charge salesmanship is that the take-charge selling must have persuasive influence on others. When you present a written endorsement of what you have to sell to a prospective buyer you arouse his interest because the endorsement is persuasive. It suggests that money can be made, or some other benefit can result by using what you have to sell. It reduces doubt by showing how somebody else has benefited. The signature of one who endorses your product has a certain persuasive selling power. In effect it says to your prospect: "Use this, as I did, and you'll be glad you did."

A verified case-record of benefits derived from what you have to sell is a potent, persuasive selling tool. It's hard for a prospect to say "No" when you lay a verified case record before him which implies: "That guy makes money by what I am suggesting that you do, and this proves it." That is take-charge selling.

When you back up verified records of others, and the enthusiastic endorsements of others, with your own personal testimony, based on first-hand observation and experience, then you have dynamic sales power in your sales situation.

A British philosopher, Sir Leslie Stephens, said this, which applies directly to persuasive power in take-charge selling:

"The only way in which one human being can properly attempt to influence another is the encouraging him to think for himself, instead of endeavoring to instill ready-made opinions into his head."

A dynamic take-charge salesman addressed a great conference of executives. He suggested to those executives that the key to their success was in picking men. He had a point there, but he didn't go far enough. He should never have limited the skill in picking men to executives alone. The key to success in take-charge selling is in picking "live" prospects. For instance, James M. Roche went from record-breaking salesman of automobiles to president of General Motors. In that climb he must have developed an insight into what causes qualified propsects to respond to the persuasive power of take-charge salesmanship. Do you suppose that Mr. Roche's ability as a take-charge salesman was not a factor in his success as the presiding executive of General Motors? Take-charge executives employ the principles of take-charge salesmanship to influence others and thereby attain their objectives.

The conversion into sales of knowledge gained of prospects is the challenge which faces ambitious salesmen. It is a persuasive challenge with the promise of lucrative rewards. By acquiring knowledge of customers and of prospective buyers a salesman with initiative and an inquiring mind can convert this knowledge into sales volume by take-charge salesmanship.

HOW TO DEVELOP PRIDE IN SELLING AND HOW PRIDE OPENS NEW VISTAS FOR DEVELOPING SALES VOLUME

Pride has dual power. It can be constructive or destructive. The form of pride which is identified with arrogance and selfishness can destroy a salesman as it can destroy anyone in any profession. But, merited pride in accomplishment and ability is something else. The latter form of pride, the constructive side of pride, is what we are concerned with here.

The authors of our best dictionaries have recognized this dual power in pride. For instance, pride is defined as: (a) An undue sense of one's own superiority; inordinate self-esteem; arrogance; conceit. And, as: (b) "A proper sense of personal dignity and worth; honorable self-respect."

The professional pride of a take-charge salesman includes these qualities:

1. *SELF CONFIDENCE.*
2. *HONESTY OF PURPOSE.*

3. *CONVERSATIONAL ABILITY.*
4. *KNOWLEDGE OF SELF, OF PEOPLE, OF PRODUCTS AND SERVICES.*
5. *WELL-DEFINED GOALS AND ASPIRATIONS.*

A simple maxim that has guided many take-charge salesmen to success is this: "Doubt whom you will but never yourself." This represents wholesome pride in what take-charge salesmanship is all about. It is a mark of sureness. It cuts through the mirage of conceit and steps out into the light of reality which thrives in the market place. It goes after sales production with vigor, crushing all sales obstacles.

You may have said to yourself: "I'll never hit the $50,000-a-year income which some salesmen enjoy." Now, ask yourself: "Why not?" It is possible. Pride in your profession is a first requirement. Confidence in your own ability to sell may turn the trick sooner than you imagine. In lieu of feeding a negative, depressing attitude, begin selling success to yourself. Change your outlook to this: "I'll top $25,000 income this year and double it next year by striking a consistent pace in selling and preparing myself to swing my volume higher each day." You can accomplish this goal by converting knowledge of markets, of products, and of people into sales volume by employing the principles of take-charge salesmanship. You can accomplish it by exhibiting pride in your work and in your product. You can use the selling power in dealing honestly and helpfully with prospective buyers. You can be more persistent, more persuasive, more creative and more imaginative.

A timid salesman I knew succeeded in freeing himself from self-depreciation and doubt and is now on top of the heap due primarily to three things: (a) he conquered fear; (b) he developed pride in what he was doing, refusing to apologize for being a salesman; (c) he took command of himself, discovered the secret power in taking command of a selling situation.

By perceptive ability the take-charge salesman recognizes when false pride tries to take control of him. To combat this he takes command of the situation and frees himself for take-charge selling. A proper sense of personal dignity, of worth, of self-respect will contribute to realizing an income of $25,000 a year, with a goal of $50,000 a year, or even the $75,000 a year which a take-charge salesman may set for himself.

Pride is an ally of legitimate ambition in take-charge selling. In its proper place pride has dynamic sales power. As Orrison Swett Marsden once wrote: "Most people do not half realize how sacred a thing a legitimate ambition is."

In its constructive sense pride is loaded with dynamic selling power and it can open new vistas for you in building profitable sales volume.

TEN NEW WAYS TO PROSPECT WITH SALES-BUILDING PURPOSE

Life insurance companies who have sold policies to me have never given me up as a prospect. They continue to send me persuasive literature with reasons why I can benefit by adding to my coverage. My automobile club has never taken a chance that I might drop my membership. The idea seems to be that while I am a member (a customer on the books) I am still on the prospect list. The department stores where my wife and I shop seem to consider us "live" prospects. Their advertising program and their sales effort within their stores are aimed at our pocket books. Every time you flip on your radio or your TV it's a safe bet that somebody, somewhere, will be actively bidding for your business. That is another phase of take-charge prospecting in action.

Prospecting can be done in various ways. Take-charge salesmen with initiative will innovate. They will devise ways to learn about prospective buyers. They will search for qualified people and they will gather facts about them with a single objective in mind: To lay the foundation on which to build profitable sales volume.

Here are ten suggestions to assist you in building a sales-producing prospect list:

1. *BECOME A FACT-SOURCE*—Study, observe and by experience become knowledgeable about products, consumers' demands, and sales problems. Do this and your reputation as a dependable fact-source will spread. You will be sought out. New prospects will be drawn to you. Then by a combination of take-charge prospecting and take-charge selling you will add to your sales volume.

2. *BECOME A FACT-HOARDER*—Gather and file pertinent facts which eventually can be converted into sales. Become a note book addict. Don't trust a fickle memory to retain

a useable fact which can be turned to your benefit. **The principle:** Clip it, write it, file it. Evaluate it frequently.

3. *SEE, HEAR AND LISTEN*—Prospect with eyes and ears at attention. Prospect constantly, wherever you are. Prospect in your club, in your casual meetings with other persons, in your formal meetings. When you hear something of interest ask yourself: "Can this be turned into more sales for me, and how?" See all, hear all, heed everything that will lead to building up your sales volume.

4. *NOURISH ALL PROSPECTS*—Devote more time and more thought to "promising" and "doubtful" prospects. Follow up by mail. Follow up with phone calls. Follow up with personal calls. Your objective: To bring lukewarm prospects into the warmth of the "live" prospect class.

5. *EXPLOIT CONSUMER WANTS*—Learn what prospects really want and why. Their wants usually are more persuasive to them than their actual needs unless they are in distress, and then they probably are not in the "live" prospect class.

6. *ENLIST OTHERS TO HELP YOU PROSPECT*—Constantly strive to build satisfaction among your customers. Satisfied customers become an army of prospect hunters marching with you. They'll enthusiastically refer you to prospects, and prospects to you, who might benefit by buying what you have to sell because your satisfied customers have benefited. This is a long-range productive phase of take-charge prospecting.

7. *CAPITALIZE ON YOUR PROBLEMS*—When you can tell a prospect that you have solved a market problem similar to his problem, you have his attention. He listens because you speak with the authority of experience. He wants to know how you can help him solve his problem. In this way your prospect comes "alive," because you have something in common with him. Each of you has a similar problem, the solution of which means more money for both of you.

8. *KNOW HOW AND WHY IT HAPPENED*—Evaluate every call you make every day. Determine how and why you lost a sale, or how and why you closed a sale. Such penetrating evaluation has a tendency to surface the underlying

facts which are vital for success in take-charge prospecting and also in take-charge selling.

9. *RELAX AND PROFIT BY IT*—Allocate time each day to play, to read your daily newspaper, your trade journals and to scan the TV agenda for the evening. In such unhurried moments you may detect more clearly things which are vital to you as a take-charge salesman, such as: product information, customer activity, market developments, new ideas, and other tidbits which, when evaluated, have sales potential. Reading, observing, clipping, evaluation is all part of take-charge prospecting.

10. *BE DISCRIMINATING*—Avoid time-wasting. Those who have not the ability to pay for what they might buy, are, in fact, time-wasters for the take-charge salesman. If credit is bad, the prospect becomes a time-waster for you. Some prospects are habitual time-wasters simply because they have difficulty making up their minds on the simplest problems. Be discriminating. Avoid wasting time on them. The alternative is to give them the full punching power of hard selling to create within the indecisive prospect an overwhelming desire to possess what you have to sell. Avoid jumping at conclusions about indecisive prospects. They may be slow to act. Many substantial accounts, however, have been developed by take-charge salesmen I have known, by patient nourishment of slow-to-respond prospects. **The principle:** Know your prospects well. Listen, see, evaluate, and *THINK.*

HOW TO ACHIEVE TOTAL COVERAGE BY TAKE-CHARGE PROSPECTING

One day I stopped at a country store and ate lunch in the coffee shop of that establishment. This was an out-of-the-way spot, off the beaten trail. This store was the trading post for quite an area. It stood alone in the center of a vast wheat-growing belt. The manager was a friendly soul. He told me about his business. He served a wide clientele of farming and ranching people. They bought in quantity. Their credit was solid. They relied on this merchant to supply their needs, not always in his line of merchandise. This far-seeing merchant went after whatever they needed or wanted if he did not carry it in stock. He told me that I was the first salesman who had called on him for months. "They just whiz by on the freeway," he said. "So I order most of my stuff by phone or by mail."

I could have considered him to be a "doubtful" prospect. But, I closed a contract with him for an advertising program by which he could maintain contact with his regular customers and with prospective buyers who might come into the area.

When I returned to my base of operations in the city I got in touch with a TV salesman. He soon established in that rural store a new TV outlet. A few months later this same salesman added household appliances to that merchant's line. Here was a prospect in the midst of market potentials which salesmen had not fully developed.

The principle: Total coverage is made possible by take-charge prospecting which explores and develops all possibilities for growth in sales volume.

A few years ago rural roads and some detours were overlooked by many salesmen as sales opportunities. Dealers and consumers on those routes supplied their needs in various ways, but the full potential for sales was not developed due to lack of take-charge prospecting. Today business is migrating from the urban areas to the suburban areas. Need for aggressive take-charge prospecting grows with this migration. Total coverage of these new and rapidly developing areas is made possible by imaginative, creative and active take-charge prospecting.

Consider these four possibilities for turning take-charge prospecting into increased sales volume:

1. *KNOW YOUR TERRITORY WELL.* Know its basic needs and its wants. Know the objectives of its leadership. Know its potentials from a sales standpoint.
2. *WORK YOUR TERRITORY THOROUGHLY.* By take-charge prospecting followed by take-charge selling. The prospect you pass up today may be the "live" one from which your competitor will get a substantial order.
3. *PROSPECT DAILY WITH TAKE-CHARGE EN-THUSIASM.* Don't hurry to get out of a producing area. Milk it dry. Haste may leave choice accounts wide open for the take-charge salesman who may be right behind you.
4. *WATCH, EVALUATE AND ACT.* Keep abreast of all real estate and building developments in your territory. Con-

structive action of any kind may hold sales possibilities for you. Investigate. That bulldozer you see in action may be the forerunner of new prospects for you. Find out what's going on. Ignoring any form of development may be costly to you as a salesman. This is take-charge prospecting.

TOTAL SALES COVERAGE involves: (a) total take-charge prospecting; (b) total know-how of your territory; (c) total knowledge of your market and its possibilities; (d) total contact with all prospects; (e) total, unceasing take-charge prospecting to make way for profitable take-charge selling.

CHAPTER TWO

HOW TO ORGANIZE YOURSELF FOR A COMMAND PERFORMANCE IN SELLING

The secret ingredient which can enable you to chart your course for "a command performance in selling" is self-discipline. From case records of successful take-charge salesmen we learn that self-discipline was the driving power which governed those success-minded salesmen in charting their courses. These records provide evidence that three steps in self-organization steered those men to success and can do likewise for you:

1. *EXERT WILL-POWER*—Victor Hugo said people do not lack strength, they lack will-power. Many salesmen have more of this strength than they realize until they challenge their own will-power in a worthy struggle.
2. *DISCOVER THE SELF-SATISFACTION IN ACCOMPLISHMENT*—A command performance in selling requires will-power, which is the essence of self-discipline. A command performance in selling becomes a reality when we arm ourselves with a positive attitude toward the task. A spirit of "this can be done" often will do the job.

3. *SELF-MOTIVATION WITH HIGH PURPOSE*—To organize yourself you require the wholesome stimulation which comes from well-planned goal-setting. Your goals should inspire you to reach up, to climb. Stimulation results from reaching up, never from stooping. It results from eagerness to engage in difficult, yet challenging sales situations.

According to Owen Meredith: "No man is the absolute lord of his life," and yet Samuel Johnson saw the problem in this light: "Self-confidence is the first requisite to greater undertakings."

The powerful motivation behind the will to organize yourself is self-interest. Boil this down and you have this: "What is there in it for me?" Stanley H. Steinway contended that to inspire workers to greater production a business house needs to exploit the self-interest of those men. "It is self-interest alone," Steinway maintained, "that will keep them keyed up to the full capacity of their productiveness."

This doctrine also applies to you as a take-charge salesman. To master yourself, to organize yourself for a command performance in selling, your own self-interest will key you up for the task.

The principle: Capitalize on the tremendous motivating power of self-interest.

In the following five points for a command performance in selling you may detect a selfish motive. It is there. It is the desire to acquire more of the good things of life. It is the desire to achieve greater personal productivity. It is the desire to gain greater rewards for better organized effort. It is the desire for leadership in our chosen field. It is the desire to become a salesman capable of taking command of any selling situation.

Are these unworthy objectives?

You have become involved in this fascinating field of selling with two purposes in mind, both of which are commendable:

FIRST, to secure more of this world's riches than you believe you can obtain by any other means.

SECOND, because you enjoy the thrill of persuading others to buy what you have to sell. From this you get self-satisfaction in swinging others to your viewpoint and this becomes part of your success plan.

Success in your purpose depends upon how well you organize yourself for your command performance in selling. This becomes a challenge to you. Take-charge salesmanship thrives on this principle of self-discipline. Here are your guidelines:

HOW TO CHART YOUR COURSE AND MAKE IT PRODUCE SALES

A management executive in the investment field made this confession to his sales staff: "I wasted the first five years in which I was engaged in this business. During those five years I marked time. Looking back at those years I now see that all I lacked was a definite, workable plan. I just had not charted a course of action to produce sales. I was making calls without specific aims. So I advise all of you to evaluate the courses you have charted. Ask yourselves if they are workable and productive plans."

The following three-way chart, simple as it is, can produce sales for you as a take-charge salesman:

1. *SET DEFINITE SALES OBJECTIVES.*
2. *DEVISE PLANS FOR ATTAINING THOSE OBJECTIVES.*
3. *PLAN TIME-SAVING ITINERARIES TO TOTALLY COVER YOUR TERRITORY AND TO GET MAXIMUM SALES VOLUME FROM IT.*

Goal-setting is a difficult job for many salesmen. They say: "Of course I have goals. I want more sales. What more is there to it?" There is much more to goal-setting than wishing. Charting a course of action is the number one requirement for take-charge salesmanship. Rudyard Kipling had an idea which take-charge salesmen might apply with profit to their business lives. Kipling said:

"I had six honest serving men. They taught me all I know. Their names were *WHERE* and *WHAT* and *WHEN* and *WHY* and *HOW* and *WHO.*"

As a suggested course for you in take-charge selling consider the following adaptation of Kipling's idea: Where are you going? What will you do when you get there? When will you begin? Why are you going there? How do you expect to attain your objective? Whom will you persuade to buy what you have to sell?

In charting your course you will discover the need for knowledge. Knowledge is the foundation of take-charge salesmanship. In take-charge salesmanship we require knowledge of people, of markets, and of products. Our take-charge sales charts are battle plans by which we propose to take command of any selling situation that we may confront. In preparing these plans we can profit by what Annie

Bessant, a noted British organizer, once said. She maintained that knowledge is essential to conquest. In the competitive battle for sales we are engaged in conquest. Annie Bessant also maintained that thought creates character. This, too, is true in selling. She also maintained that character can dominate conditions. Many take-charge salesmen have tested this principle. They have found that in many sales situations character creates circumstances as well as environment favorable for developing sales volume.

One industrialist who came up through the sales route pointed out that salesmanship and advertising contribute to the capital worth of the firm if salesmanship and advertising have the character which creates or increases good will among customers for the firm and for its products.

All of this reflects the attitude of salesmen. In the overall sales objectives of the course which we have charted to produce sales in volume, attitude is important. Attitude is flexible. Golden K. Driggs, another business executive, stressed the point of flexibility of attitude. He said: "If you don't like a situation change your attitude." There is one key to success in many fields. Attitude requires a certain commitment to a course of action. It calls for decision. Mind-wandering is foreign to take-charge salesmanship.

An advertising salesman floundered for months until he found the key to getting business. This man sold advertising book matches. When it dawned on him that he was not selling matches but an advertising, sales-producing medium, he made more calls with enthusiasm and produced more sales. This man also saw that businessmen could use more calendars and ball point pens than he was selling if they became convinced that these items could be converted into sales production. As a result he built up sales volume by selling advertising as a profitable investment for businessmen and using ball point pens, calendars and book matches as vehicles for reaching potential customers.

When this salesman discovered the simple principles of take-charge salesmanship his attitude changed and his sales volume gained. He succeeded in organizing himself for a command performance in selling by charting a productive course of action. In doing this he also discovered that multiplication intrigued him. The multiplication in take-charge selling applies to any line you may be selling. It is simply the charting of a sales plan which develops a number of sales where only one sale had been produced before.

HOW TO TAKE CHARGE OF YOUR FEARS AND BECOME A TAKE-CHARGE SALESMAN

Frightened salesmen may be rare but you still meet a few in the market place. These nervous, indecisive individuals can, and many of them do, succeed by taking command of their fears.

A case in point is a woman from Texas who took command of her fear of selling and succeeded. She confessed that she was "scared to death" when she made her first call on a business executive to talk about advertising. She told of how she capitalized on her fright by turning it into courage. This is how she did the about face: She said that each order she wrote renewed her courage. In time this thrill of accomplishment became more powerful than the restraints of fear. She said that when she realized that she had been afraid of meeting "the nicest people I have ever known I became ashamed."

What, then, is the fear which holds some sales people back? What fears do you have that limit your sales production? Again we have the need for self-examination. Check the following list. See if it contains your basic fear. Identity may help you defeat that fear which has been robbing you of your capability to sell more:

1. *FEAR OF MAKING A MISTAKE.*
2. *FEAR OF FAILURE.*
3. *FEAR OF FACING UP TO PEOPLE OR TO A PROBLEM.*
4. *FEAR OF TAKING A STAND, OF DEFENDING YOUR CONVICTIONS.*
5. *FEAR OF EMBARRASSMENT.*
6. *DOUBTFUL OF YOUR OWN ABILITY.*
7. *FEAR OF CRITICISM.*
8. *FEAR OF THE CHALLENGE TO SELL A TOUGH PROSPECT.*
9. *FEAR OF LOSING PRESTIGE.*

If the ghost that is making you fearful or doubtful is not included in the foregoing list, identify that ghost and conquer it by courageous, positive action.

A veteran salesman in the construction industry assures us that ghosts of fear and doubt work on prospects as well as on sales people. He pointed out that we often overlook the productive side of fear. He referred to case records which disclose that fear motivates buying in situations such as these:

1. Fear is a motive in buying life insurance.
2. Fear is a motive in buying hospital insurance.
3. Fear is a motive in buying accident insurance.

Such fears are exploited by take-charge salesmen.

A prospect's fear of leaving loved ones penniless if death should snatch him from the scene is a powerful motive for buying life insurance.

The danger of having a prospect's income shut off, or his cash reserve depleted by sudden illness or injury, is a powerful motive for buying hospital insurance.

The horror to a prospect of anticipating that he might be the victim of an automobile accident, of being unprepared to defend himself in a damage action, or of being unprepared to pay for damage to his car and for personal injuries, constitutes an overwhelming motive for him to buy automobile or other accident insurance, as well as liability insurance.

Take-charge salesmen in those fields exploit such fears, and legitimately so. They can exploit such fears with clear conscience because they are inducing others to protect themselves from disaster. This is take-charge selling.

When fears grip a salesman he need not give up. He can do something positive to combat the fear. Case records support the effectiveness of this method:

Number one among remedies for conquering unreasoning fear which haunts many salesmen is to take charge of your fears. Face up to the situation. Adjust to things and conditions. Strive to understand people and their peculiarities.

The principle: Be flexible. Master your fears and exploit the fears of prospects.

A field salesmanager in the cookware field said too many new men joining his sales force are afraid they may blunder if they aggressively move into a selling situation. He said he often calls to the attention of these fearful men what Elbert Hubbard once said: "The greatest mistake you can make in life is to be continually fearing you will make one."

This suggests that fear fosters greater fear. It is also true that courageous action fosters greater courage. Positive action clears the way for becoming a take-charge salesman.

A former victim of fear who has topped sales records in the home furnishing industry relates how he handled the fear problem. "I stopped fighting the problem," he explained. "To magnify fear only makes it worse. I found that the solution was to act; to do something positive. I was among the most fearful of salesmen when I began," he admitted. "I defeated fear by forcing myself to move into the most hotly contested selling situations. Each experience gave me renewed strength. Finally I discovered that I was enjoying the conquest. Shyness left me. Fear left. My sales volume got bigger."

A million-dollar-club insurance salesman declared that fear in selling is simply a suggestion to the fearful salesman that success can't happen to him. His remedy: "Take the opposite track. Convince yourself that the toughest prospect on your list can and will be sold by you."

Ernest Hemingway told a group of sales people at Sun Valley one night that "if you expect failure you will have it." And what did Hemingway know about selling? He wrote books and they sold in quantity. And what did he know about failure? He experienced it many times. Nevertheless he conquered his fears and succeeded in his profession.

HOW BOLD SALESMANSHIP TAKES CHARGE OF DIFFICULT SELLING SITUATIONS

Few things can rock a salesman out of a sales slump as quickly as one of his colleagues asking him: "What has softened you? Who has taken the ginger out of you? A month ago you were cashing in on the bold approach. Now you have become meek and timid. And, your sales are down. How come?"

One of America's great life insurance companies recently published an impressive advertisement; impressive to take-charge salesmen. The ad showed a training instructor standing between a blackboard and a television screen. A statement and a question appeared on both the blackboard and the TV screen. The message was: "You couldn't sell him! *WHY?*"

I recall a young man who was challenged when a man he knew threw in the towel and quit his selling job. He said: "Nobody can sell our high-priced products in those hick towns." This grabbed the young man. He promptly went after that job. He became determined to prove that he could sell high-priced quality food products in that rich rural area. He succeeded so well that he became the district sales manager of the firm. His pitch: The enjoyment of the better things in life, not the price of the product.

Bold selling requires persistence. When Calvin Coolidge was president he had a lot of political "selling" to do. He said: "Nothing in the world can take the place of persistence."

A newspaper advertising salesman succeeded in developing a non-advertiser into a large-space advertiser. When he was asked how he convinced this hard-to-sell merchant that he should change his ways of merchandising the salesman listed these three points:

1. Bold presentations to show how others in the prospect's line of business were gaining in sales volume by using newspaper space wisely.
2. Bold salesmanship to win the confidence of the stubborn prospect. This established free communication between prospect and salesman. To this new ideas for developing greater sales volume for the prospect produced results.
3. Persistence, which is the process in bold salesmanship which has the power to penetrate the armor of the most determined resistance.

J. Paul Austin, a lawyer who turned salesman and became president of the Coco-Cola company, told his colleagues that he learned to sell as a route salesman on Coke trucks. His technique was bold salesmanship. He developed the technique of bold selling of ideas in face-to-face confrontation and also speaking platform. Witness this from one of his speeches:

"The art of successful selling, and it is an art, is more mysterious than the workings of a computer—but the results—well, the results can be beautiful, baby—absolutely beautiful."

Your next drink of a certain popular beverage testifies that bold selling has made it "the real thing."

HOW TO PLAN CALLS TO PLACE YOU IN THE TAKE-CHARGE DRIVER'S SEAT

Salesmen whose calls are expected by prospects and are also anticipated with some degree of expectancy are in the take-charge driver's seat upon arrival.

A pharmaceutical salesman built a reputation of being an "idea man." He made it a practice to bring something new in merchandising methods to his customers and to new prospects. His calls were welcomed. His prospects were in an expectant mood when he arrived. This reduced sales resistance to a low ebb.

A promotion-minded salesman who built volume in carpet sales brought sales promotion ideas to his prospects of all sorts of home-furnishing products. He created a favorable climate for selling by directing his prospect's thinking into profit-making channels.

It has been demonstrated that four keys to planning calls assist in placing salesmen in the take-charge driver's seat. The four keys:

1. *CONCENTRATE ON SELLING MORE*—A salesman carrying widely diversified lines profits by concentrating on related items. Instead of splashing his whole line before a prospect he concentrates on a few related items. When sales are closed on these related items he introduces other groups of related items. This take-charge salesman's record shows that by concentration his sales per order have increased and his total volume gains steadily.

2. *MINIMIZE THE LONG-HAUL, LOW-PROFIT CALLS* —By concentrating more calls in one area and covering it well the take-charge salesman avoids time-wasting jumps to here and there. Salesmen sell only in the presence of prospects, not on the freeway straining to get to one more prospect before closing time. **The principle:** Concentrate on take-charge planning.

3. *MAKE PERSUASIVE PHONE APPOINTMENTS*—Sales records in a multitude of lines disclose how profitable persuasive phone appointments can be. For instance: "Mr. Smith, I just received something that is going over in a big way. It's new. I'd like you to have the first look at this and give me your appraisal of its market value. How about nine o'clock tomorrow morning? O. K. I'll be there." There's a touch of persuasion in that call. The prospect is left with anticipation.

4. *SET DEFINITE GOALS*—Sales figures tell the story on this. Goals do have motivating power on salesmen. An office supply salesman said he stepped up his volume by setting a goal of more volume per call. An investment salesman says he sets a new, but attainable goal, every month. "I just don't like to admit to myself that I can't make a goal that I have

set for myself so I put in extra steam to make it and usually exceed my monthly goals."

The principle: Plan calls to produce greater volume per call. Set up attainable goals. Commit yourself to reach the goals you have set up for yourself. Have an alternative for each sales objective, just in case the No. 1 idea fizzles.

HOW TO DETECT TRICKS THAT ARE DESIGNED TO DERAIL YOU

Tricksters are among the difficult prospects with whom salesmen must contend. Don't underrate those tricksters. They have an objective: to derail you before you can create a desire in them for what you have to sell. If they succeed, they're happy. Their sadistic success feeds their ego. But, some salesmen do capitalize on such trickster attempts by skillful take-charge salesmanship.

Out of case records we get a close-up view of some of the tricks which have been sprung on salesmen in various fields. Let's examine them:

1. *THE QUICK COMPLAINT*—Fault-finding probably is the most transparent of the tricks that will be thrown at you in an attempt to throw you off balance. As Robert West, business executive, once pointed out: "Nothing is easier than fault-finding; no talent, no self denial, no brains are required to set up in the grumbling business." Case records show that take-charge sales people capitalize on complaints, accepting them as opportunities. One such salesman presented his own "A, B, C" plan for capitalizing on complaints: (a) Avoid arguments. (b) Forthrightly accept responsibility and quickly switch the complaining prospect's (or customer's) attention to your efforts to rectifying whatever, from the prospect's (or customer's) viewpoint, may be wrong. (c) Thank the complainant for bringing the matter to your attention. The "thank you" has a disarming influence. It has a mellowing influence. Often, "thank you" can establish a favorable selling climate.

2. *THE BETTER PRICE TRICK*—The counter-attack weapon for the low-price trickster is to agree with him, according to a salesman of wide experience in the wholesale women's wear lines. This salesman said that after quick

agreement with the low-price trick he moves at once into a quality demonstration, ignoring the price. He concentrates on value and style and consumer appeal. This take-charge salesman has found that price objections which may be sincerely made can be handled by breaking the price down to unit cost. He, too, believes in praising the price-complaining prospect for his desire to want quality. This tends to disarm may price-complainants. Direct questions are effective in countering the better price trick. This simple question has been used by many take-charge salesmen with favorable effect: "Why do you feel that this product is overpriced?" If your prospect gets specific in his reply then you have something tangible to work on. His reply, said this salesman, may provide you with an opportunity to become a take-charge salesman in fact by convincing him that your product is a good value.

3. *THE "WE NEVER HAVE A CALL FOR THAT" TRICK* —This trick is a challenge to take-charge salesmen. In fact, it is an invitation to take positive selling action. One salesman in the coffee industry demonstrated how to take charge of a situation such as that. When a prospect told him that he never had any call for his brand of coffee the salesman proposed to show him that "calls" for the coffee could be developed. The prospect was in a mood to be shown. The salesman prepared a special window display and served free coffee in the prospect's store. The result: A large order, a happy customer, and the seed was planted for market development of his brand of coffee. Profits resulted for both salesman and merchant by positive action by a take-charge salesman.

4. *THE "QUICK SWITCH" TRICK*—Many indecisive prospects are masters of change-the-subject technique. They respond with a blank stare when a salesman speaks to them and then they take off on an unrelated discussion. One advertising salesman in the broadcasting field developed an effective way to get such prospects back on the track. He listened to the prospect's off-trail discussion and, on the first break, he used the prospect's own technique against him. He ignored the subject the prospect had been talking about and asked a provocative question: "Did you hear what happened

to your friend in business over on Tenth Street?" The surprised prospect responded with, "No! What happened to him?" To this the take-charge salesman replied: "Well, he took on spot announcements in the TV show I've been talking to you about and his sales on carpet have gone up 25 percent in the last two weeks." Result: The "quick switch" to derail this salesman failed and the take-charge salesman worked out a contract for TV spot exposure for this prospect.

5. *THE LOYALTY TRICK*—This trick is a favorite with the chesty type of prospect. Usually he is a self-satisfied individual. This may be your first or second call on him. He puckers his lips and says: "I think we are both wasting time. We buy from salesmen who have sold to us for years. We stick with our friends." The intent, here, of course, is to deflate you, but take-charge salesmen have ready answers for this sort of trick. A diamond and jewelry salesman I knew ran up against this sort of barrier. He praised his prospect for being so loyal. "I've heard a lot about your loyalty to salesmen," he told his prospect. "I assume your loyalty has paid off well for you." He told me that he immediately noticed a fresh glint in his prospect's eyes. "Paid off for me?" the prospect questioned. "Of course," the salesman replied. "I came in today to suggest that we could place an exclusive line with you that could boost your total sales volume to a new high. Now, does that interest you?" The salesman said the jewelry merchant cleared his throat and replied calmly: "Why, yes. Of course I'm interested if there's money involved." With that this take-charge salesman got down to serious business. By that time the jewelry merchant had forgotten about loyalty. The take-charge salesman had switched his thoughts to greater volume and profits.

The principle: Tricks to derail you can be converted to sales by ingenuity and take-charge salesmanship.

HOW TO PROFIT BY WRITING YOUR OWN TICKET

This is the pay-off step in organizing yourself for a command performance in selling. To take this pay-off step you need to know where you are going and how you propose to get there. You need to know those two essentials if you would succeed in take-charge selling and if you would enjoy the rewards of writing your own ticket.

At the distinguished award ceremonies honoring an outstanding real estate salesman, that honor-winning salesman said: "There is no magic in selling. It requires work, intelligent planning, and enthusiasm. With this combination plus study and a genuine liking for people you can write your own ticket. I did. I wrote my own tickets by setting my own objectives. Only twice did I fail to reach my objectives. The reasons for those two goof-offs became clear to me when I examined my own record: (a) insufficient foresight in planning; (b) lukewarm attitude; (c) lazy working habits."

In a survey of how sales leaders in various industries succeeded in writing their own tickets, four essential requirements stand out as guides for becoming take-charge salesmen:

REQUIREMENT No. 1—More planning, more perceptive planning, more creative planning . . . *PLUS* more ambitious goal-settings, more realistic goal-settings, and greater awareness of your own capabilities.

REQUIREMENT No. 2—A thirst for progress. A driving ambition to rise above yourself and achieve greatness . . . *PLUS* a personal commitment to do so.

REQUIREMENT No. 3—A refusal to quit or to accept half successes. A spirit of self-motivation that establishes big-ticket value on the virtue of stick-to-it-iveness.

REQUIREMENT No. 4—The daily look in the mirror—the daily self-examination; the daily self appraisal; the desire to detect and examine your own errors; the will to recognize those faults and to correct them; the "hot" desire to recognize your own capabilities and your own strong points and to determine how best to capitalize on them.

HOW COMMAND SALESMANSHIP CAN UPGRADE YOUR STATUS AND YOUR INCOME

This is an exercise in self-evaluation.

If you open a prospect's door and meekly confront him, you place him in the driver's seat and you have lost command of the situation . . . but, if you step into his office with a firm step, with a smile of confidence lighting up your face and you challenge him with a bold statement, you have aroused interest in that prospect. I recall a salesman who walked into my office and opened up on me with this statement: "I have an idea here which may be able to add 15 percent to your gross income next month." What happened? I listened. That salesman had an interested prospect on his hands and he knew it. He went on. He spoke firmly. He spoke with authority. He told me and he showed me how easily I could probably add 15 percent to my gross income in the next thirty days. He produced rather convincing evidence that what he was saying was true. I bought that set of books. That salesman had whetted my appetite for making a few extra dollars and I was converted to the idea that I could swing that by investing a few dollars in a set of books. That was take-charge salesmanship. That salesman upgraded his status as a salesman. He knew his business. He was bound to upgrade his income.

Because success in take-charge selling depends to a large extent on frequent self-examination, the following chart has been helpful and profitable for other salesmen.

Take-charge salesmen who are consistently increasing their sales volume agree that frequent self-appraisal keeps them on their toes. It enables them to organize themselves for a command performance in selling.

Use of the personal status-rating chart is a tested and effective method of sizing up your own performance in take-charge salesmanship. When used with a sincere desire for self-examination it may contribute to your next successful command performance in take-charge salesmanship.

MY PERSONAL STATUS-RATING CHART

Designed for Frequent Use to Upgrade
Incomes of
COMMAND SALESMEN

ASK yourself these questions: (Answer honestly and with personal courage)	Occasionally	Frequently	Always	Never
Do I display sureness in selling?				
Do I show willingness to right a wrong?				
Do I seek opportunities to do a good turn?				
Can I support what I say?				
Do I take command of sales situations?				
Do I speak with authority?				
Am I positive or arrogant?				
Am I persistent or stubborn?				
Am I agreeable or a "yes" man?				

CHAPTER THREE
================

HOW TO USE COMMAND SELLING SHOWMANSHIP IN YOUR SALES CALLS

A salesman in the construction equipment business entered a conference room in a Pacific coast city to present a proposal to the executive committee of an expanding real estate development enterprise. This was his first experience in trying to sell to a mass audience. He quickly realized that his problem was similar to selling to an individual except that he had the challenge of converting many instead of one. He also realized that he had to quickly capture mass attention, that one inattentive person in the group might distract others in the group. To capture this mass attention he combined showmanship with his sales presentation.

Opening his case before the audience, he brought out a small mechanized model of a new development in loading equipment. He put this model into action on the big conference table. That did it! Those executives around that conference table began reaching out to hold, to handle, to examine a "toy" in action which suggested more profits for them in their business. By take-charge showmanship this take-charge salesman had set the stage for a dynamic and sales-producing presentation.

Another take-charge salesman, representing one of the nation's leading airlines, made this point:

> The basis of any effectiveness in a sales pitch is the salesman's own point of view. To sell, he must believe in what he has to sell. He must believe that it can benefit in some way the prospective buyer. He must be able to show how it will so benefit the buyer. This may call for a dramatic presentation.
>
> The first step the salesman must take is to do something to grab the attention of his prospect. Then he must stir up interest in what he has to sell. I do this by using what I call a "gimmick." This is my method of showmanship. I try to make my presentation dramatic. My objective is to set in motion those interesting points which will, hopefully, lead to a sale. Air travel and air freight is my business. Those provide me with a wide range of possibilities for capturing interest and creating desire within the prospect. I have found that if I have succeeded in developing strong interest in my product, and if I maintain momentum in my presentation, never allowing it to lag, that in due time I will wind up with profitable results.

The idea that showmanship has an important role in take-charge salesmanship isn't altogether new. For instance, the side-show barker was a central figure when the circus came to town. He filled the tents with paying customers by employing the magician's art, by breathing fire, and by other methods of showmanship.

Armies have been recruited by showmanship. Volunteers for service became sold on the patriotic theme and on the prospects for adventure and opportunity for advancement.

Little-known products have suddenly taken hold in the market place because some take-charge, salesminded person took command of the selling situation and promoted those products by showmanship in demonstration, in person-to-person selling and in advertising.

Take-charge showmanship is a companionate, persuasive force in take-charge salesmanship.

HOW TO DETERMINE YOUR MOST EFFECTIVE APPROACH

Take-charge selling requires:
  (a) An estimate of the selling situation.
  (b) A plan to capitalize on the situation by an attention-arresting, convincing approach.

The knowledge you have previously gained of your prospect lays the groundwork for your estimate of the situation. This knowledge will sharpen your skill in prejudging situations and sales problems involved.

A top producing, take-charge salesman in the investment field pinpointed his various successes in this way:

> A skilled public speaker seizes the attention of his audience by a direct, challenging thrust. I have found the direct thrust to be effective in selling. I lose no time when I get in to see a prospect. I go right after his attention. I do this by using some form of showmanship. I believe that my mission is to make a stronger believer out of my prospect than I am myself, if that is possible. To do this I may have to pour currency out of a bag, or pull a rabbit out of a hat, but I must do something to grab and hold that prospect's attention. If I can dramatize money-making possibilities by pictures, I use pictures. If I can back up my claims for my product by graphs and charts, I use graphs and charts and dramatize them. I am convinced that showmanship, constructively used, is an effective method of booming sales. If I act like a clown and by so doing get business, then I do a bit of clowning. My whole objective is to get my message across in such a way that it produces sales.

A paper-products salesman who succeeded in developing sales volume in what had been condemned as "dry" territory attributed his success to attention-arresting approaches in his presentations. "The straight pitch has been my most productive approach," he said. "When you hit people directly with something that means a benefit for them, you're bound to get attention. I try to get right to the point about how they can make money by buying what I have to sell. I have yet to meet the man who isn't interested in making a fast buck. If showmanship will do it, I go for showmanship." He then broke his selling technique down in this manner:

(a) The straight pitch arouses interest, gets attention.
(b) The straight pitch involves the prospect. It presents to him an idea by which he can profit.
(c) Showmanship puts fire and action into the straight pitch.
(d) Hammering away on the prospect's opportunity to benefit keeps the prospect thinking along a predetermined line which is intended to lead the prospect to a decision to buy. This is best accomplished by dramatizing all the possibilities open to the prospect for profits and other benefits.
(e) Showmanship and the direct pitch should attain their max-

imum impact at the crucial moment of decision, when the sale is either made or lost. This is the moment to maintain control of the selling situation. The approach should have laid the groundwork for this closing moment vitality. It should have accomplished this by a constructive flash of take-charge showmanship which energized the entire sales presentation.

HOW TO DEVELOP A COMMANDING ATTITUDE AND GENERATE GREATER SELLING POWER

We were in the sofa-bed area of a high-volume furniture store when a smiling, out-going young salesman introduced himself. Promptly he went after our attention by showing us the "new colors," and the "new designs" and he made much of the "newest thing" in almost indestructible fabric upholstering. My wife and I were mildly startled when this take-charge salesman picked up a switchblade knife and drove the blade into the cushion of one of those beautiful sofa-beds. Then he invited my wife to examine the "wound." Dramatically he pointed out that the fabric was not injured by the knife blade, that the fabric did have self-healing qualities, and he had proved it. This was showmanship with a flash and with take-charge attitude that generated selling power. He sold the lounge to us by take-charge salesmanship seasoned with showmanship.

To be productive a sales presentation requires objective planning. It should have these four essentials:

1. *CAPTIVATING INTEREST.*
2. *STRONG, CONVINCING QUALITIES.*
3. *TEMPTING, PERSUASIVE QUALITIES.*
4. *STIMULATING QUALITIES TO CREATE DESIRE TO POSSESS WHAT THE SALESMAN HAS TO SELL.*

The sales representative for a chain of high-class motels which bid for convention business listed eight points for sales planning which he called his "power-structure bid for business." His eight-point take-charge plan follows:

1. Use short words. Use short sentences. Make it clear.
2. Use showmanship and voice inflection to add emphasis and selling power to your presentation.

3. Choose strong words. Use words of action.
4. Know your product, know its uses, know how it can benefit the buyer.
5. Be authoritative. Speak as an authority on the subject. Use simple, understandable language.
6. Use colorful, meaningful examples and demonstrations. This is showmanship of a high order.
7. Prove your claims. Cover all the bases. Leave nothing in doubt or open to question.
8. Put showmanship into repetition. Repeat persuasive points often enough to assure that you have attained maximum selling impact.

Words can become "killers" in a sales pitch. One of such words is "expense." Take-charge salesmen avoid using the word "expense." Instead they talk about how to turn the products they sell into profits, or comfort, or other benefits for buyers. They use "investment" instead of "expense." There is an element of showmanship in this sort of straight talk. Most important, however, is that it stimulates a desire to buy.

One salesman told a group of his colleagues that he had experimented with a negative approach to nudge a hesitant prospect to act. It worked. This salesman sold investment properties. He said to his prospect: "If you are in doubt about this deal being a good investment for you, take my advice. Don't buy it. I wouldn't want to be a party to adding to your worry or to what you are fearful of being an expense to you." With that the salesman said he began closing his brief case. The prospect stopped him. "Let's take another look at those figures," he said. The salesman again went over his proposal. This time the prospect became convinced. He bought. By subtle showmanship the salesman had shifted the problem to the prospect. He had taken a risk and he had won by an "I don't care" approach, which implied, "It's up to you." This was subtle showmanship—take-charge showmanship. It was also a take-charge attitude. And, it was take-charge salesmanship.

HOW TO SHOW AND TELL WITH COLOR AND CONVICTION

A dynamic speaker was also a volume-producing salesman. Repeatedly he had swung individuals and audiences to his viewpoint on a variety of subjects. The secret of his persuasive power was that he showed and told with color and conviction.

This take-charge salesman devised a system of evaluating newspaper advertising. His objective: To make print advertising more productive in sales. He tested his system. He became so fully convinced himself that he reduced doubt about this form of advertising to a minimum. Then he launched his own campaign to sell his system to newspaper publishers. He cooperated with his client-publishers to assist them in selling the basic idea of his system to those who bought space in the newspapers. This, he claimed, would develop more selling power in advertising and would therefore yield higher dividends to the advertisers. This, of course, would persuade them to use larger space, which would increase the total advertising volume for the newspaper publishers.

When this dynamic individual's idea was distilled it was not complicated. He simplified it. He made it attractive, with qualities which promised greater returns for those who bought his idea and made use of it. His three-point sales technique was this:

1. Show the No. 1 prospect (the publisher) how he could benefit profit-wise by training his own advertising staff to assist potential advertisers to prepare more productive advertising.
2. Show and tell the publishers and their prospective advertisers how to go about getting more sales from their advertising.
3. Present factual evidence of results obtained from advertising prepared in accordance with his evaluation system.

Demonstration is the effective method of convincing a prospect that he can benefit by using your product. Demonstration is the "show" method. When you show and tell with color and conviction you have a dynamic sales combination.

If your product is such that it can be given movement (animation) for the demonstration, then it takes on a greater quality of interest. The prospect sees more clearly how your product applies to his needs or his desires.

The graph or chart is an effective "show and tell" device. You can "talk to" these sketches, pointing out how certain effects illustrated there apply to your prospect and to his business. You add sales impact to a graph or to a chart when you present it with a flourish. Doing this, you have added showmanship to your presentation. All of this combines to provide a "tool" for a take-charge salesman to clarify his idea, to add importance to his product, and to generate selling power by adding strong conviction to his presentation.

Pictures which are made graphic by the use of overlays increase their selling power. The picture plus the overlay can show a buyer how your product can benefit him by showing him how it has benefitted others. Pictures which show the product in use add the selling power of movement (showmanship) to the display and enhance their selling power.

The sales director of a large department store told a group of his sales people in women's wear and the men's shop: "Without color and without pictures showing our lines your individual sales would take a nose-dive. I suggest that you study each fashion ad that we publish or that we use on TV. Use the fashion ideas that are stressed in those ads. Point out to your potential customers the newest creations from the fashion centers of the world. Get them interested. Get them talking about what we have to sell here. Have a copy of our latest ad handy so you can use it in talking to your prospective buyers. Those pictures and those printed words and what was shown on TV last night make what you say so much more convincing."

That's good advice for any take-charge salesman on the road. Know what your house is doing to promote the products that you sell. Then show and tell with color and conviction, and profit by this whole combination of sales power which can build your sales volume.

Pictures, charts and graphs provide take-charge sales people with something tangible, something believable, something vivid to talk about in the presence of a prospect.

An organ dealer created an effective on-the-floor display around a chord organ. His blown-up picture display showed a man who was having fun fingering the organ. This gave him an opportunity to point out to a prospect that he, too, could have fun with a chord organ whether or not he knew anything about music. His pitch was that in a matter of minutes the prospect could actually be producing tunes.

Asked why he put so much effort into promoting the low-priced chord organ, he replied:

> There's more color and conviction in this than in a professional instrument. I'm striving to get those without musical

training to become interested in organ music. If I can convince one of them that in a few hours he can be playing tunes it won't be long until he will be wanting to talk about a real organ. Every person I can get to sit down and try this chord organ expands my live prospect list. The more colorful I can make this display and my presentation, the easier it will become for me to get people to sit down and try to play. When they do sit down and I can show them how they can actually get music out of this instrument without having had musical training, I'll have them involved. And, once they find out that they can handle this little organ, some of them are going to reach out to seriously tackle organ playing. Then I'll get them to study with us and that will lay the groundwork for big ticket sales.

This enterprising music dealer developed sales volume by this step-up show and tell idea which was aimed at prospect participation, conviction and decisive action. That's take-charge salesmanship!

HOW TO CAPITALIZE ON YOUR PROSPECT'S GREATEST INTEREST—HIMSELF

Recall the mirror trick? That guy who stares at you out of the mirror each morning is your primary concern for today.

Every prospect you meet today is likewise interested primarily in himself whether or not he was stared at by a fellow looking out of a mirror, which he probably was. To that prospect *HE* is his No. 1 concern.

Your challenge as a take-charge salesman: To find a way to capitalize on that man's interest in himself. Doing that, you will have solved one problem of upgrading your sales volume.

How then can you capitalize on another man's interest in himself? There are several possibilities born out of the experiences of top producers in selling. Let's examine a few of those possibilities:

1. *CAPITALIZE* on a prospect's discontent.
2. *CAPITALIZE* on a prospect's success.
3. *CAPITALIZE* on a prospect's slump in business.
4. *CAPITALIZE* on a prospect's fame.

Let us examine some case records on how we can capitalize in such instances:

A salesman for a well-recognized home-study school encountered a low-spirited discontented man. This man was young. He obviously had some ability. A brief interview disclosed that he had many worthy aspirations. His discontent indicated that he had the will to protest against his own lack of progress. He grumbled to the salesman that "the breaks have been against me." The salesman decided that at that moment that man was in no mood to digest what the salesman had to say about the opportunities awaiting him through self-education. Two days later, however, that salesman sent that discontented young man a telegram. From another town that salesman wired: "Just received some important information which can mean a more prosperous future for you. Will be back in town in a week. I'll see you then."

That telegram from another town in that situation was a flash of showmanship. The discontented young man now was shaken out of his low spirits. He had been fed with bright anticipation. The fact that someone had become interested in his welfare had sales impact. This salesman had taken charge of a difficult sales situation. Where there appeared to be no prospect, this take-charge salesman had created a "live" one. "I enrolled that fellow on my return trip," that salesman told me. "Two years later I saw him again. He was happy and prosperous in a new field which I had a part in opening up for him. The way I look at it, his success was a sort of bonus compensation for me in that sale.

The principle: When a discontented prospect paints a dark picture for you, be patient. By take-charge salesmanship you may change that prospect into a "live" one, by capitalizing on his discontent.

The sales representative for a packing material house had a tough-to-land prospect in mind. Repeated calls had failed to get this man on the books of the house. One day that prospect scored a victory in a golf tournament. The salesman read about it. He was at that prospect's office the next morning. He made a special trip out there to congratulate the tournament winner. This placed two men interested in golf on common ground, except the prospect was a champion. They talked at length about golf. Gradually the take-charge salesman steered the discussion into money-making. The tournament winner was also interested in making money. This time the prospect became a customer for that salesman. An alert take-charge salesman understood what a taste of fame could mean to a man and he capitalized on it.

An interior display salesman profited by capitalizing on a business slump. He made a good customer out of a poor prospect by presenting sales-building ideas to him with take-charge showmanship.

An insurance salesman capitalized on the fame of a local political celebrity by suggesting that good business dictated that he should be more adequately covered.

A vast field of opportunity for service and profit exists for take-charge salesmanship, fortified by take-charge showmanship, in capitalizing on the greatest interest of prospects—their own welfare. Charles Dickens once suggested: "Possibly we might even improve the world a little if we got up early in the morning and took off our coats to the work."

The knack of using take-charge showmanship in sales calls, and coupling it with an insight into the objectives of our prospects in order to capitalize on their self-interest, is the magic fuel which can propel sales volume to higher levels. That fuel is the secret of the success of many take-charge salesmen who "reach for the skies" and attain their high sales objectives.

HOW TO MAKE YOUR ORDER BOOK AN EFFECTIVE PROP IN TAKE-CHARGE SELLING

An energetic young salesman in the air conditioning industry thrust this idea into a discussion at a sales seminar:

"How many of us here use our order books as sales props and how effective have we found this to be?"

Response to his question was spotty. There was evidence that the question had shock effect on some of the the salesmen. One salesman spoke up: "I keep my order book in the bag until I feel sure that I have the business in the bag."

Another salesman had a different slant on this idea. He said: "I get my order book out early. I feel that if I place the order book on my prospect's desk at the beginning of the interview, it's handy to get at when I need it. I usually slip something over it to conceal it from full view. I feel this eliminates any possibility that the order book might distract the attention of my prospect during my sales pitch."

A tire salesman who has a high production record was in the field when I interviewed him. He was more enthusiastic than the seminar crowd over the selling power in an order book. He said he brought his order book out first thing in an interview with a prospect. "I lay it on his desk so he can get accustomed to seeing it. I have found that my order book does two things," this salesman told me. "First, the order book arrests attention. Second, the order book is bound to stir up thoughts of buying in the prospect's mind."

This salesman cited several cases in which the whole trend of the selling process was changed by pulling out the order book at the right moment in closing the sale. "The moment would have been right," said this salesman, "had the order book been on the table, but it was not. The salesman had to pull it out of his bag, exposing it to the prospect's view for the first time. This caused the prospect to reconsider while the salesman was fumbling with his order book, getting carbons in place and getting all set to write the order. The prospect lost his buying fever. He decided to put off buying. By strong selling effort the salesman succeeded in getting a modified order out of the prospect—much less than the original order might have been. Had the order book been before the prospect from the beginning of the sales presentation there would have been a good chance that he would have not changed his mind. I have found in my experience that the order book, placed on the desk of a prospect as one of the first props in a sales presentation, becomes a familiar object and, as such, has sales value. The moment the prospect sees your order book he either thinks about buying or about how to get out of buying. As you progress with your interview you try to lead your prospect to concentrate on what you have to sell and to its possible advantages to him. So when buying time comes the order book is there along with your samples and other props in selling. In this way it seems to me that the order book contributes to a successful close."

The order book has been aptly called a "silent salesman." Take-charge salesmen in a variety of situations claim this to be true. Case records indicate that silence itself often becomes a forceful selling factor. Take-charge salesmen use this technique. For instance, a business machine salesman at times placed his order book on a prospect's desk and then supplemented its silent selling influence by using the art of silence at the right time. In one instance he handled a difficult prospect this way:

"Look at this list of accounts," he said, displaying a sheaf of orders. "These buyers of this same type of machines I am showing you are in the same business as you are. They make money by equipping their offices with these modern, time-saving pieces of equipment. Now, would you be kind enough to explain to me why you should not profit in the same way that these men profit. You know many of these men. You know how well they are doing." With that, this salesman stopped talking and remained silent. He moved his order book a trifle, just enough to call attention to it being there. The order book had been there so long that it had become familiar to the prospect. Now the salesman wanted to suggest buying and he did so by just shifting the position of the order book. The silence in that sales situation was broken by the prospect. He had arrived at a decision—a decision to buy. And, the order was written in the book that had been used as a selling prop.

Hazards do arise to devitalize sales presentations. Early exposure of the order book need not be one of those hazards, as some salesmen may fear. If the sales presentation is to be successful, then eventually the order book must come into the picture. Take-charge salesmen who have tried the early exposure technique believe it has sales power. It makes the order book part of the selling process from the beginning. It becomes as familiar to the prospective buyer as one of the samples or documents that occupy a spot on the table beside the order book. The order book becomes a positive suggestion to buy or not to buy. The salesman takes it from that point. The order book becomes one of the props by which he can close a sale by take-charge salesmanship.

The principle: Take-charge salesmanship employs every conceivable device to produce a buying decision by the prospect. New, colorful, persuasive ideas are employed. Each is employed to take the prospect by the hand and lead him to the order book—the "silent salesman." The silent order book can be and has been effectively used for take-charge showmanship in making take-charge sales calls.

CHAPTER FOUR

HOW TO TAKE THE FIVE VITAL STEPS FOR ATTENTION-GETTING PRESENTATIONS

Once again, the exploiting of self-interest becomes the key to success in take-charge salesmanship.

The Steinway family manufactured and sold pianos. They understood the value of exploiting self-interest. Their success in marketing their product and in exploiting the Steinway name as a symbol of quality testifies to their ability to manipulate the key to success in take-charge salesmanship. Charles H. Steinway made this observation about self-interest as a motivating force:

"I cannot commend to a business house any artificial plan for making men producers—any scheme for driving them into business-building. You must lead them through their self-interest. It is this alone that will keep them keyed up to the full capacity of their productiveness."

Self-interest is a double-edged sword which, when wielded by a skilled take-charge salesman, can motivate him to top his previous sales records day after day. At the same time self-interest creates within prospects an irresistible desire to buy what the take-charge salesman has for sale.

Five vital steps are involved in capturing the buying attention of prospects:

STEP No. 1—"I have an idea by which you can benefit" becomes your battle cry. This reaches out and penetrates your prospect's sale-resisting armor.

STEP No. 2—Now you have your prospect's attention. Now you hit him hard with compelling reasons why your idea means cash dividends for him or that those reasons mean something else of great value to him, such as pleasure, fun, popularity, easier living, or greater prestige.

STEP No. 3—To capitalize further on your idea you now dissect it. Piece by piece you show your prospect the built-in value to him of your idea. You strive to convince him that your idea vitally concerns his personal welfare.

STEP No. 4—You now back up everything you have said and everything you have shown to your prospect about what you have to sell with easily understood facts. You present endorsements of your product or service. You offer alluring and convincing examples of how others have invested in your idea and have come out ahead in the deal.

STEP No. 5—This is the moment of decision. You maintain buying pressure, gently but firmly persuasive. You bring all the enticing goodness of your idea together for a final parade of inducement to motivate your prospect to say "yes." By take-charge salesmanship you help your prospect to make that decision, recognizing that decision-making often is painful for many people. When sales-resistance is at low ebb you move in for a dramatic close, leaving your prospect with the good feeling that you have been his benefactor.

An idea, loaded with self-interest for your prospect, is the key to getting attention for your presentation. An idea, too, is the key to successful take-charge salesmanship.

HOW TO CAPITALIZE ON BULL'S-EYE SELLING, THE TECHNIQUE OF TAKE-CHARGE SALESMANSHIP

Bull's-eye selling is the opposite of shotgun selling. It is concentrated selling, and when that principle is activated by salesmen who are themselves sold on the idea, bull's-eye selling produces sales in volume.

I recall when I almost lost a piece of business by failing to have a central idea in mind for my sales call. Lacking this, I just gabbed with the manager of a brewery. He was a pleasant fellow. When I was about to walk out empty-handed he said: "By the way, my truck salesmen need something for a door opener. If you see anything that might be suitable let me know."

That fellow set up a bull's-eye for me to shoot at. This simple act revived me from a lapse in take-charge selling. I had key cases in my line and those key cases had bottle openers in them. I suggested to the brewery manager that if those key cases were imprinted with the brewery's trade name, they would be appropriate for his trucker-salesmen to present to prospects in lieu of business cards. I sold him on the idea that the key cases would be more substantial for a truck-driver to present than a dainty card. He went for the idea. The sale was substantial. But it provided tangible evidence to me that bull's-eye selling does pay off.

The alternative to bull's-eye selling is shotgun selling. In shotgun selling you dump a bag of samples on the desk of a prospect and say to him: "There must be something in all of this to appeal to your trade." There's little punch in that approach. Experienced buyers say that decision-making becomes difficult when nothing is featured. This frequently occurs in sample rooms. These buyers prefer to judge from groups of related items. They admit they respond to bull's-eye selling—concentrated selling. The single idea approach which we call bull's-eye selling is used by successful take-charge salesmen in many lines. It is based on the principle of selling an idea rather than on selling items.

One chain of hamburger stands zoomed its volume by bull's-eye selling. Instead of promoting just hamburgers it promoted "barn-busters"—a giant-size burger with sauce and trimmings included.

A lumber company aimed a sales campaign at a single item and shot sales skyward on that item by bull's-eye selling. They featured toilet seats for that campaign. The attention-getting idea that one salesman came up with was this: Concentrate one-week's sales effort on toilet seats, promote them as "the best seat in the house." The idea sold hundreds of toilet seats for that lumber company. In addition, the attention-getting idea drew new prospects to the store and these prospects were sold other merchandise by take-charge sales-manship.

Insurance salesmen who receive the coveted keys to the million-dollar club get there by bull's-eye selling. They concentrate their persuasive fire on an idea which provides a protective cover for their prospects. It's the idea that has selling power. Not all prospects become excited about buying insurance but they are vulnerable to an idea which shows them that insurance will benefit them.

A small, foreign-import car shook up the American automobile market by bull's-eye selling. The selling plan even capitalized on what the makers of this car exploited as "ugliness." This got attention. This sort of take-charge salesmanship developed volume by bull's-eye selling. The sales appeal was concentrated on an idea, not on so many pounds of steel. Selling power was aimed directly at "the bug," and it got through to those who would plunk down the low purchase price and would move the car off the sales floor and get it into freeway traffic.

To capitalize on bull's-eye selling in your line, do this: (a) dig deeply for a "big idea" that will make your prospect sit up and take notice because your idea promises benefits to him; (b) sell your "big idea" by seeking out live prospects who can benefit by buying your product; (c) become over-sold yourself on your "big idea" so your enthusiasm for it will affect every prospect you contact.

HOW TO DEFINE YOUR TARGET AND MAKE IT PERSUASIVE FOR YOUR PROSPECT

Much as a take-charge salesman might define his target, the apostle Paul, addressing himself to the Philippians, set up his goal. Paul made his target persuasive. His message to the Philippians was this: "One thing I do, forgetting those things which are behind, and reaching forth unto those things which are before, I press toward the mark." As sales people, endeavoring to influence people, we need to clearly define our objectives. Our goals, which are our targets, should be in the future if we are to become successful take-charge salesmen. In selling, pressing toward our mark becomes an exercise in goal setting for it is selling with a single objective.

To define your target do this:

1. Clearly state it. Write it down. You might ask yourself if your goal is to sell more tomorrow than you did today. If so, how do you propose to reach that goal. Or, you might ask if your goal is to move into new territory and gain a

foothold there for your product. If so, by what strategy do you propose to accomplish this task? Or, you might ask if your goal is to develop a new class of customers for your product, and by what means do you plan to reach your objective? In any case your success depends largely on how well you can define your target.

2. Clearly state your plan of action. Be specific. Make a promise to yourself that you will do this: (a) make a gain in sales volume of a specified amount by a fixed time or date; (b) or, in new territory which you propose to exploit, that you will concentrate your sales effort on selected prospects. Name those prospects. Definitely plan how you propose to win those prospects over to your customer-list; (c) or, that you will concentrate on selling your product to a select class of prospects (naming them) and that your plan for taking them into your camp is constructively developed. (Before you execute your plan ask yourself if you know enough about your prospects. Specifically, how do you propose to develop sales volume in new territory? How do you propose to do so in your present territory?)

3. Know where you are going and why. Know whom you intend to see and why. Know how your product can beneficially affect those whom you intend to interview.

4. Learn more about your product and its uses. Learn more about your prospects and their lines of business. In each instance clearly define your target and how that target can be productive of sales for you.

A printing salesman examined his sales over a period of several months and discovered that his orders were becoming too similar. He concluded that if this trend continued he would eventually become known among his clients as "the man we buy our shipping labels from," or "the man who takes our orders for office forms and stationery." The outlook disturbed this salesman. He recognized a threat to his growth as a creative and productive salesman. He recognized that he was drifting away from creative selling and was slipping into a gulf filled by peddlers. This, he vowed, would not happen to him. Reversing his selling procedure, he set up a fresh target—to sell more to those who were now buying from him. He proposed to do this by presenting new ideas to them, such as how their image could be improved by more impressive stationery. This required planning. It required getting art ideas. It required take-charge salesmanship. Working along this line he produced a persuasive idea, and he sold it with art sketches and a presentation which suggested ways which would enhance the prestige of his client. When he had attained this objective of selling an idea in stationery improvement, he came up with ideas for improving office forms and direct advertising material. These ideas caught on because he exploited them and made them persuasively attractive to his prospects.

The printing salesman was typical of those who recognize that to clearly define a target is a major step toward shifting from the slow pace of order-taking to the exciting pace of take-charge selling with its greater rewards.

HOW TO DEVELOP THE ART OF TURNING TIME-KILLING INTO SELLING

Time-saving is the antidote for the poison of time-killing. For instance, consider the sales-building possibilities in the following suggestions for saving time:

1. You are a busy man. It's profitable for you to become known as such. Time means much to you. You do "mind waiting" to see your prospect. When you are asked to wait this often means an indefinite wait. Faced with this situation you can turn a time-killing possibility into a selling opportunity by pressing for a definite future appointment and get on your way to sell to someone else. This is part of take-charge salesmanship. It has proved to be profitable for other take-charge salesmen. And, when you press for a specific appointment, go after a key person in the firm, someone who has the authority to make a buying decision.

2. As a take-charge salesman you must be a foe of procrastination. You fight this tempting "bug." You recognize that the put-it-off habit is treacherous, that it is a thief of time—selling time. Therefore you avoid getting hooked by "tomorrowitis." Instead you cultivate the "do-it-now" habit. You face up to your problems. You do something about them—*NOW!* By nourishing the action habit you defeat the time-killing habit and stimulate a desire to sell more, *NOW!* Charles E. Wilson, the industrialist, made this point about taking action: "People who fail to achieve what they want in life don't want it badly enough to do the hard work. There just ain't no golden chariot that will take you there."

3. As a take-charge salesman you plan tomorrow's calls today. This cuts down on lost time resulting from starting the day without a definite objective. It avoids time-killing, a product of catch-as-catch-can sales calls. Lack of planning is the vicious time-killer. Thorough planning is the time-saver. Thorough planning is the constructive force which builds sales volume. A text book salesman told me that he spent one evening on one project—to prepare himself to make one effective presentation the next day. "I devoted four hours to constructive planning to achieve that goal," he said. "The result was that I landed a contract which I had been after for several weeks."

4. As a do-it-now take-charge salesman you schedule your tough prospects for early morning calls. At the beginning of the day you are fresher, more alert, perhaps more persuasive. Those tough prospects probably are less frayed in the morning than they will be later in the day. They may even give you a more cordial reception first thing in the morning than they will after they have been bombarded with problems throughout the day. In case record after case record we find that salesmen make better headway in tough situations in the morning than later in the day. If this proves to be true for you, then early morning calls on your hard-to-convince prospects can be chalked up as time-savers for you, and more productive, too. . . . The sales manager of an industrial development complex made this point to his sales crew: "You'll notice that I try to spring the unpleasant things on you in the morning. I have found that you are more receptive and more pliable at 8 a.m. than you are at 5 p.m. My principle is this: Get the unpleasant things out of the way so I can get on with the productive work that has to be done. I have also noticed that salesmen who refuse to dodge tough prospects and, with determination, go after business from those tough prospects, usually succeed in getting sales volume."

5. As a take-charge salesman you probably favor what one dynamic sales executive called the "ten-minute-early habit." This take-charge sales executive said that his most productive salesmen were those who were 10 minutes early for his sales conferences. "They appear to be eager to get the most out of the conference, to get problems solved, and to get back to selling. Their sales records tell the story. Those men sell. They dislike killing time. These men are among the early birds when they make calls on prospects. They arrive ahead of time for their set appointments."

6. In the class which we call take-charge salesmen you break away from the "linger longer" group. A high-producing business systems salesman confessed to a group of his colleagues that he had to break the "linger longer" habit. "That one is a time-killer," he admitted. "When a sale is closed you have the perfect setting for saying 'good-bye' with a smile, a 'thank you' and a fast get-away. This type of time-saving for you and for your prospect, or customer, usually is approved by busy business people."

Thomas A. Edison devoted odd moments, so often wasted, to thinking, to planning, and ultimately those odd moments were converted to inventions for the benefit of mankind. Edison's ideas are still being capitalized on by take-charge salesmen for the development of sales volume.

Thorpe B. Isaacson, an educator who turned his great energy to the insurance business and chalked up high sales volume as a salesman and as a sales executive, was a respecter of time. As he saw it, "the proper use of time has helped many young men and women to greatness."

One of the challenges in take-charge salesmanship is to develop the art of turning time-killing into selling. The moments we kill could be more profitably spent in the presence of a prospect. Thoughtful planning, realistic goal-setting, dynamic action, are all allied with the art of turning time-killing into sales volume.

HOW TO TURN TAKE-CHARGE SELLING POWER ON YOUR PROSPECT'S WANTS

This is the key question to be answered by take-charge salesmen with some degree of self-assurance:

Why should this prospect buy from me what I have to sell?

There are two points in this question: (a) "Why should the prospect buy from me?" And (b) "Why should the prospect buy what I have to sell?" Both of these points which are involved in a sale require the persuasiveness of take-charge salesmanship.

On the right answer to the foregoing question rests the success of virtually all sales interviews. Let us consider some of the many wants, desires and other motives for men and women deciding to exchange their money for something else:

1. *COMFORT*—A strong selling point. People do yield to the persuasive power in the possibility of enjoying easier living for themselves and their families.

2. *MONEY-MAKING*—The desire to become rich or richer has wide appeal. The urge to get one's fingers into the "pot of gold" can be capitalized on. The craving to bring a great dream into reality makes a prospect vulnerable for a well-planned sales presentation.

3. *SECURITY*—The longing to be free from the threat of material losses. It involves freedom, lack of freedom, poverty and riches, safety and disaster.

4. *FEAR*—The desire to fortify one's self and loved ones against preventable disaster.

5. *HEALTH*—The desire for freedom from disease, to prevent disease or to have health restored.

6. *PLEASURE*—Most prospects will part with their money if you can assure them that they'll have pleasure or fun in doing so.

7. *STATUS*—The urge to raise one's self above himself; to attain position; to achieve success; to be noticed; to win the acclaim of those in high position; to elevate one's standing among friends and even within his own household; to become more charming; to become more impressive in action, in conduct, and in appearance.

8. *LOVE OF OTHERS*—The desire to improve the lot of family or friends; to shield them from hardship; to comfort those in distress; to provide them with an economic umbrella at his own expense.

9. *POSSESSIVENESS*—The common desire to have what someone else has for pleasure, for profit, for security, for status-building, or for self-satisfaction.

10. *BEAUTY*—The compelling desire of many to improve their personal appearance, to become physically attractive to others.

The foregoing wants of prospects were taken from notes of a top-rated salesman in the investment field. "Those 10 compelling wants of average men and women set up 10 targets for me to shoot at," this salesman explained. "Those 10 wants (and no doubt there are many more) motivate me to dig, and dig, and dig to find out as much about a prospect as I can. If I am to sell to him I need to know what he wants out of life and how badly he wants it."

Now that we have 10 suggested targets we have a well-defined objective for take-charge salesmanship. We have 10 tips on how we may gain a prospect's attention. We have 10 tips on how we may be able to persuade him to buy what we have to sell. It is time now for us to evaluate our own take-charge sales power and see how well-armed we are to zero in on the 10 targets of desire which we have set up. Here are some fundamental requirements which have been time-tested for productivity:

COURTESY—Be polite, but firm. One hard-driving sales success in real estate worked by this rule: "Show your teeth if it's necessary, but smile when you do so."

SPUNK—This is the spirit of courage and should not be confused with arrogance. One of my sales supervisors put it this way: "The selling power in spunk derives from the salesman's knowledge of his product and how it can benefit his prospect." An account executive for a large advertising agency told his sales staff one morning that spunk had merit. He said: "Even the most difficult prospect, in his determination to keep you from winning him over to your point of view, admires polite spunk in a salesman." The top executive of one of our major accounts made this appraisal of a spunky salesman the other day: "If my men had the spunk of that salesman we would dominate our market."

KNOWLEDGE—Go in armed with knowledge of your product, of your prospect and of his business. Back up your facts with evidence to make your presentation click. A master in training salesmen in the home-furnishing industry offered this warning to a large group of sales people: "Anything you say can be used against you by a prospect unless you can support what you say with factual evidence that is convincing to that prospect."

SPEAK UP—Speak clearly, concisely, convincingly. You may kill the sale by "beating around the bush." **The principle:** Get to the point quickly. Hammer away on your prospect's self-interest. Keep in mind that the prospect is primarily interested in himself.

USE VISUAL AIDS—Pictures, graphs and charts can support

your main selling thrust by adding conviction to what you say. Use visual aids as selling tools, not as a crutch.

ASK, ASK and ASK—Take-charge selling includes the power of suggestion. With the order book in sight of the prospect it becomes a natural for slipping in the suggestion to buy. Do this often in your presentation. A young insurance salesman came back to the office after an experimental call which he had been assigned to make. The sales director asked him: "How many times did you ask that fellow to buy?" The young man blushed. "I guess I forgot all about that point," he replied. **The principle:** Ask, ask and continue to ask for the order. Take-charge salesmen succeed in building sales volume by telling, showing and asking for the business.

HOW THE MAGIC OF A FRESH IDEA GENERATES TAKE-CHARGE SALES POWER

A fresh idea may be the product of experience, study, self-motivation and the enthusiasm of seeing the idea become real and grow in influence. Someone likened an idea to a piece of ore, requiring prospecting, digging, analyzing and evaluating. An idea may turn out well or it may disappoint you as the ore did with the prospector who had unearthed "fool's gold."

Dale Carnegie had the idea that he could train men and women to sell and that he could train them to develop sufficient self confidence to succeed by "thinking on their feet." His idea blossomed into an enterprise that has touched the lives of thousands.

Stanley H. Slotkin saw the possibilities in having useable things for hire. He established a firm called "Abbey Rents," and by take-charge salesmanship he piloted his idea to success. Slotkin is said to have called himself the "highest paid salesman" on the enterprise he created.

Harold Sanders—"Colonel" to you, sir—got an idea that better fried chicken could be sold in greater quantity. He knew how to produce better fried chicken. He combined his formula and his process with the franchise idea and sold "Kentucky fried chicken" franchises on a royalty basis. This required vision, knowledge, self-confidence, guts and the enthusiasm of take-charge salesmanship.

The magic of a fresh sales idea comes alive when its power is generated by liberal doses of self-motivation, by captivating simplicity, by the impressiveness of humility, and by the persuasiveness of plain talk. Salesmen who have discovered this magic have learned the secret of effective communication. They "rub elbows" with people in all stations in life to find out what makes them tick. They have mastered the art of being "good company."

Walter P. Chrysler placed excitement ahead of enthusiasm when it came to selling automobiles. "When salesmen get excited they get customers excited and we get business," Chrysler said.

Charles Schwab, who was intimately acquainted with success in the market place, attributed his success to enthusiasm. Whether we call it excitement or enthusiasm, it amounts to an emotional drive which makes us hungry for action. An emotional drive can set a man on fire when he comes up with a fresh idea in which he has faith that it can boom his sales record. Mark Twain characterized an emotional drive as excitement.

When a take-charge salesman becomes excited over his idea it is not unusual at all to see that man's sales volume go up and up. The magic of a fresh idea breeds excitement, and this same magical force can activate selling power within spirited take-charge salesmen with fresh ideas.

CHAPTER FIVE

HOW THE THREE-POINT TEST CAN ENERGIZE YOUR SELLING POWER

Self-evaluation is the fuel with which the three-point test energizes your selling power. In this test we look at ourselves and we ask questions. We stand alone at this testing point to "do our thing." Let us now examine this three-point test to which we are asked to submit ourselves for honest self-appraisal:

1. *Did You Capture Your Prospect's Interest at Once?* (Think back to your last sales presentation, whether that was the sale you closed or the one you lost.) In today's furious competition talk is not enough to capture and to hold a prospect's interest. When you self-examine your last successful sales presentation it is quite probable that you did three things to make it successful: (a) you told; (b) you showed; (c) you retold. The third point, the "c" point, is most important. You retold those captivating facts about what you had for sale. You told and you retold those facts. By retelling you became more dramatic. By dramatizing those facts you keyed up your prospect's enthusiasm over what you had for sale.

I know a salesman who has often publicly thanked his dad for teaching him how to profit by doing more showing than telling to capture a prospect's interest. This salesman retired leaving an enviable record of profitable take-charge salesmanship. "I was eight years old when I made my first sale," he said. "My dad was a photographer. He also knew how to sell his product. Our town was buzzing with activity that day. Veterans of Indian wars were meeting in a regional convention. Dad made souvenir buttons to sell. Each button carried the picture of a 'respected' Indian chief. Dad pinned those buttons on the bib of my overalls and sent me out to show off what I had to sell. This act of showmanship caught the attention of my prospects. One old-timer pointed at the picture of an Indian chief on the bib of my coveralls and said: 'I had one chance to shoot at that guy and I missed him.' He bought a button from me. His pals bought more buttons. They stripped the bib of my overalls of buttons. I had to return to my dad to get restocked. I have profited many times by that experience. It taught me the value of doing something right away to get attention if you expect to make sales."

Salesmanship has moved up a long way from the days of the "drummer." Today salesmen are professionals. We become take-charge sales people by improving our sales techniques. Doing this, we discover that it is possible to boost our sales higher than we had ever dreamed possible.

2. *How Persuasive Have You Been in Convincing Your Prospect that He Should Buy from You?* (Recall now that self-interest is the surefire bid for interest in what you have to sell. To achieve concentrated attention you relate what you have to sell to the needs and wants of your prospects.) For instance, an industry has been built in greeting cards by making an appealing, self-interest pitch to persuade prospects that they should buy a certain specified greeting card to make sure that "when they care enough they send the very best."

A young, aggressive, and thoughtful salesman grabbed the attention of parents by reminding them that the text books he sold contained the secrets for the future progress of their children. "The kids won't give a hoot for these beautiful covers," he told the parents, "but they will care for all the goodies in the way of knowledge that are between these covers and they will care for what it can do for them in their lives." He hammered away on that point until parents believed that their children would profit by what those books offered.

This salesman capitalized on the desire of those parents to do something constructive for their children. Doing this, he captured their attention. "When I began closing sales," this salesman declared, "I began to realize that there was more than kid-appeal involved. Those parents suddenly had become proud of what they had bought. I saw that I had fed them self-satisfaction as a topping for their self-interest. And, the way they reacted seemed to convince me that I had become the one guy who could provide them with the benefits that were in those books for their kids."

3. *How Convincing Have You Been that Your Prospect Will Personally Benefit by Buying Your Product and Buying from You?* A colleague of mine was a facts-and-figures salesman. And, he was a good one. That take-charge salesman got right down to serious business with his prospects. He threw convincing facts at them to show them how they could benefit by buying what he had to sell and by buying from him. Facts and figures were the energizing elements of his sales strategy. He dramatized those facts. He made facts "come alive." He shunned dullness and deadly routine statistical presentations. And, when he succeeded in exposing a point which aroused interest in his prospects, he let go with the full force of his selling power.

One high potency take-charge securities salesman gains his maximum sales momentum by motivating prospects to talk about themselves. "When a prospect opens up and tells me about his hopes, his dreams, his personal problems, and even his fears, he opens up for me a vast field of opportunity," this man declared. "Often I win two ways in such situations. I not only make a sale but I also enlist a friendly booster who provides me with fresh tips for additional business possibilities."

Most of us who tote briefcases, sample cases and presentation kits can profit by putting ourselves on the spot and subjecting ourselves to regular and critical self-appraisal. When a prospect loosens up and talks to us about himself he is doing two things: Unwittingly, he is doing his bit of self-examination. He is also subjecting us to a fresh view of ourselves. It just might be that he is exposing some of our sales weaknesses, too. Whenever our prospects open up it's a challenge to us to listen attentively.

In the three-point test we have a simple method of digging into our own treasure chests of personal qualifications. Such self-examinations energize many salesmen and cause them to uncork sales power which had been dormant for want of motivating fuel. The simple three-point test has proved its effectiveness in many cases. By giving it a serious, determined try-out ourselves we may find out just how we stand with ourselves. We can take a cold, poker-player's look at our last sales presentation and dare ourselves to decide whether it was really the best we could do. Honestly, now, how would you rate yourself?

Each of the three test points have one thing in common. The three points have a single purpose. They are designed to prod us into fully revving up our selling power. They are designed to concentrate the spotlight on our goals so we can get the whole depth of the picture clearly in mind. Those three points in the test are designed to *sell us* on the idea that we ought to get with it and fully cash in on our take-charge selling power.

WHEN DID YOU BEGIN CLOSING THE SALE AND HOW DID YOU MAKE OUT?

A former colleague of mine who has become known among salesmen as a "go-getter" had the following ready answer for the question which is posed above:

"If I begin to close when I first open up on my prospect and maintain that closing attitude throughout my sales presentation, I have little worry about how I am going to make out."

This is more than an apt reply to a vital question. The "go-getter" amplified his reply with this observation:

> I begin closing right at the start by shooting at my prospect with a statement that affects him personally. For instance, if I assure him that he can double his profits in six months by taking on what I have to offer him, I am pretty sure that I have started wheels turning in his head. I have his favorable attention, which is the number one accomplishment in selling. Moreover, I have created an atmosphere favorable to selling because this man is definitely interested in making profits out of what I have to sell. Right off the bat this lays the groundwork for closing the sale in due time. The secret of closing is simply this: Begin at the beginning and stay with it. My own sales records prove this principle to be sound.

A young man who moved into the take-charge selling class early in his career appeared before the sales promotion board of a large corporation. He went into the conference room fully confident, because he was well prepared. He had a plan. "Our competitors were pouring it on this account," this salesman later explained. "They argued that they were entitled to first claim on the account for some reason that seemed to me to be hazy. They made their play on what they called factory capacity, larger inventories, high industrial rating, and other claims of greatness. It seemed to me that their bid for the business was based on their self-interest. So, I reversed the approach. I went after the business on the basis of the self-interest of those to whom I expected to sell. At the outset, without any reference to the competitor's proposal, I made a pitch on why the firm which the board represented would profit by taking on our products. From the opening of my presentation to the moment of closing I hammered away on the consumer demand we had built up through our extensive advertising campaign. I showed the board how we had developed a ready market for them to supply. I supported my statement with solid documentary evidence. By starting out on this theme and clinging to it the close was not complicated. I left that meeting with the signed contract in my pocket."

Salesmen close sales by taking charge of sales situations. By taking charge at the outset they are in better position to maintain direction all the way to the close. An orderly presentation, with closing as the goal, involves five steps:

1. *Appropriate showmanship*—An attention-arresting opener which involves the prospect in possibilities for realizing desirable benefits.
2. *The show-and-tell technique*—Heightening of interest in what we have to sell and also in our integrity. All this to create confidence in us and desire for what we have to sell plus willingness to do business with us.
3. *More show and tell*—Dramatization of what we have to sell and its dramatic possibilities for benefiting our prospects. Suggest or speculate on profitable initial quantity or date when service should begin—a subtle way of getting the prospect to think about buying.
4. *Concentrated selling*—Develop sales points which we noted registered most favorably with our prospects. Discard nonproductive elements in either display or presentation. The closing moment draws near. Bear down on desirability of acting now in the interest of the prospect.

5. *It's buying time*—Our order books should have been out in view of our prospects during our presentations. This reduces "shock" in opening an order book. Be helpful to prospects in their decision-making problem. The close should come naturally if we have maintained sales momentum, holding our prospects' interests in the spotlight throughout.

The mechanics of closing a sale need not be painful.

The principle: Make everything very clear and very easy for your prospect to buy.

Closing may be a critical moment even for a take-charge salesman. The salesman is somewhat in the position of a physician in whom a patient has confidence to the point of decision. For instance, the physician finds it necessary to "sell" his patient on the "desirability" of immediate surgery. Some physicians are masters of this art. They become super-salesmen. They are in the take-charge salesmanship class. They get near to their patient (their prospect). They win his or her confidence. Take-charge salesmen also work closely with their prospects to win their confidence in themselves and in whatever they have to sell.

In each sale we close and in each sale we lose, certain mysterious ingredients are present. It is profitable for sales people to identify those ingredients. We probably can identify the sales strength we brought to bear on our prospects to motivate them to buy and to buy from us. Each sale involves that dual persuasive force. Why is this true? No doubt it is due to what most successful take-charge salesmen call "planned selling." Self-examination will convince us that sales seldom just happen. They are planned to succeed. The emotional appeal you make to supplement your factual presentation may often prove to be the ingredient which swings the reluctant prospect to say "yes, I'll go for that." The emotional appeal is closely linked with enthusiasm in selling.

An automobile salesman with a climbing record told his colleagues on the sales staff that he had found that emotional presentations built sales volume for him. "At first I snickered at the idea that a guy could get emotional over a load of steel. I soon got wise, however, to the fact that women buy cars. They can get very emotional over new cars. When I invited a woman to get behind the wheel in one of the luxury jobs I saw what emotion can do in making a sale. I got that woman to fiddle with the gadgets and to run her hands over the rich, soft seats and the swank interior finish. You can bet she got emotional. In fact, I got emotional, too. I got excited about that car. I built up its luxury qualities with enthusiasm. Of course I put over the deal. I closed the sale and got on with the job of getting emotional all over again in order to sell another car."

HOW TAKE-CHARGE SELLING CAN RELEASE YOUR HIDDEN PERSUASIVE POWER

When you hitch up dynamic leadership to take-charge salesmanship you throw open the gates and release your hidden persuasive power. This fattens your bank account, enriches your life, and motivates you to reach out for higher achievements.

Take-charge salesmanship is leadership of a special quality. The principle of take-charge salesmanship is this: To establish yourself in leadership position in every selling situation.

Here are three dynamic ways to sell:

1. Immediately get favorable attention of your prospect.
2. Immediately go after creating desire within your prospect so he or she will want to possess what you have to sell.
3. Motivate every prospect to act in a way which you suggest will be in his own behalf—to buy what you have to sell.

Goal-setting is a vital thing in take-charge selling. For instance, a young man set up two goals for himself: Goal No. 1—To become a successful lawyer. Goal No. 2—To become a successful salesman in order to finance his legal education. Both goals were positive goals. No half-way effort would attain this young man's objective either in Goal No. 1 or in Goal No. 2. Both of these goals were success goals. Both of these goals were alluring and they were attainable. Law was his *BIG* goal. Take-charge salesmanship was his *BIGGER* goal. Take-charge salesmanship had to carry a double load. He had to succeed in selling to insure his success in the law.

With this challenge to his own self-confidence this young man plunged into the competitive insurance field and he succeeded. He became known in business circles of his community as a leader in estate planning. His hidden persuasive powers had been released by take-charge salesmanship which shoved him into leadership position.

He entered law school armed with that same zest which caused him to *THINK BIG* in selling. He "moonlighted" throughout his college training. He maintained a leadership position in estate planning while he was chalking up "A" grades in law school. And, when he had passed the bar examination, he had a metal plate placed on his office door which read: "Attorney-at-Law and Counselor in Estate Planning." He welded two professional achievements into a dynamic combination which released more of this man's hidden persuasive power.

Adam S. Bennion, a utility executive and leader in education, possessed qualities which motivated others to "reach for the sky" in commendable pursuits. Of leadership, which is so vital in take-charge salesmanship, Mr. Bennion said: "The first price you pay for leadership is a thoroughly sound grounding in what I call preparation. No great leader ever became a great leader in eight hours. If you want to be comfortable take an easy job. If you aspire to leadership take off your coat."

One morning I listened in on a leader in advertising and promotional selling. He was "taking off his coat" and he was urging his listeners to do the same. He chalked some intriguing figures on the board. "These figures," he told his audience, "represent a few bold steps I had to take to achieve the sales volume goal I had set up for myself. I want each of you to set up your goals and meet with me again one week from today. At that time I am going to ask you by what means you propose to reach your goals. I challenge you to be prepared to answer that question with a sound plan of action."

Another sales leader in the heavy construction equipment industry discussed "born salesmen" with me. He said: "When I went into selling a lot of fellows told me that salesmen were born, that I couldn't get anywhere by dreaming that I could make good in selling. They said that if I hadn't been born to be a salesman it wouldn't work out. I went ahead and proved that those guys were cockeyed. Of course, I knew that a salesman had to be born, but I didn't believe that men are born to be salesmen or musicians, or what have you. Yet, that is what those fellows were trying to make me believe. Funny thing, too, a lot of men I know use that as an excuse when they don't quite measure up in selling."

That take-charge salesman expanded on his point of view: "I try to think big," he said. "I believe that successful selling requires certain positive attitudes. I plan to succeed, never to fail and never to just get by. I set up goals for myself. In doing that I also set up alternative routes to reach my goals just in case I run into road blocks along the primary route. My whole operation is based on the principle of succeeding."

Take-charge salesmanship holds out all the challenges which have proved so motivating, so strengthening to those who have become great sales leaders. It has released their hidden persuasive powers. One such salesmen in the field of "bank service selling" quoted Orison Swett Marden at a sales convention. Marden once said: "Most people do not half realize how sacred a thing a legitimate ambition is."

Ambition is the product of inspiration, motivation and perspiration, according to some of the most successful sales leaders on the road today.

In seriously considering how take-charge selling can release our hidden persuasive powers we are confronted with the ever-present problem of rough roads ahead. We are also stimulated by the prospect of smooth highways along our route to success in selling. But, it becomes necessary, if we are determined to succeed in take-charge selling, to take into account the ambition-killing obstacles that are bound to show up. Let's identify enough of those to get us on fighting terms with them: (a) tension; (b) doubt; (c) boredom. We can be assured that this trio will conspire to keep our hidden persuasive powers suppressed.

The energizing factors which have the power to cause us to reach for high level successes in sales volume include these:

(a) *BIG THINKING.*
(b) *BOLD* selling.
(c) *MEANINGFUL,* persuasive presentations.
(d) *SINCERE,* persuasive talk.
(e) *SUCCESS*—planning and thinking.
(f) *SELF CONFIDENCE.*
(g) *SELF-MOTIVATION.*

To release our hidden persuasive powers we need to get on intimate terms with the foregoing seven success factors in take-charge selling.

HOW TO PROFIT BY A SWITCH IN PACE FOR TAKE-CHARGE SELLING

Luther H. Hodges, former secretary of commerce, and prior to that an executive in the textile industry, challenged salesmen to profit by what we are now calling a "switch in pace." Mr. Hodges put it this way: "Innovation and salesmanship have to stride forward together to keep a free enterprise economy moving toward ever higher levels of prosperity."

We have, as a nation, industrially created new and improved products. We have accomplished this largely by innovation. With the zeal of take-charge salesmanship we have generated mass consumer demand for those products.

A specialty salesman once demonstrated how we can go about profiting by a switch in pace. This man had been told that physicians were ethically beyond his reach as prospects for this products. One of his friends warned him that ethical doctors say "no, no" to any idea that smacks of advertising. The specialty salesman's creative mind challenged this bugaboo, and he knocked on the door of a busy pediatrician. The waiting room was filled with impatient mothers and whimpering children. The specialty salesman got the immediate attention of the doctor by this straight-forward pitch: "I have something here that will pacify children, even in a doctor's reception room. I'd like to show it to you when you can spare 10 minutes. It isn't a new thing but it is something that will make kids want to come to see you." The doctor took 10 minutes away from his waiting patients to look at the salesman's samples of toy balloons. He listened to the salesman's idea: To imprint the balloons with this message: "A gift from the doctor to one of his best young friends." The salesman's point was that this was not advertising, per se. It did not even mention the doctor by name. Yet it had good-will-building power over the kids, and over their mothers, too. The salesman maintained that it would be strictly ethical for the doctor to do what he suggested. It would simply be "a nice thing to do." The doctor "bought" the idea. The salesman had broken down a barrier. He had sold advertising balloons to a non-advertising prospect by a switch in pace, by innovating, by take-charge salesmanship.

To innovate means this to take-charge salesmen: (a) To make changes. (b) To bring in something new or new ways of doing things.

George Romney, former governor of Michigan and a take-charge salesman in his own right in the automobile industry, tossed this challenge to other salesmen:

"There is no virtue in what we call 'consistency' as it is usually understood. Flexibility—the willingness to change with changing conditions—is essential in this dynamic and progressive world."

To achieve maximum results from take-charge salesmanship we

find merit in the following suggestions from a woman who climbed to high volume status in the insurance field:

1. "Learn something new every day. Get wide knowledge. Venture into strange places. Meet people in those strange places. Listen to them. Learn to better understand them. Learn more about their needs and their wants."

2. "Eye those strange places and the people in them with a single thought in mind: 'How can what I have to sell benefit this place and/or these people?' This will often call for a change of pace. It may call for innovation, for creative thinking. It calls for imagination of a high order. It calls for deep and sincere interest in people, for there, before you, is your market."

We can also profit by a change of pace in closing sales. The sales director of a large development operation declared that too many sales are lost by what he called "a fade-out at closing time." He said: "When our men relax at closing time it shows up on the consolidated sales reports for the day. It's easy to pinpoint the low-pitch closers."

Another sales executive with a record of high production himself and a man who places great emphasis on his training program for salesmen, projected this formula for closing a sale:

  (a) Switch from pressure on your prospect to magnifying the desirability of your product.
  (b) Blow up your prospect's wants. Glorify his desires.
  (c) Whet his appetite for what you have to sell by making it mouth-watering.
  (d) Make him hungry enough and he'll buy with minimum personal pressure.

One of the sure-fire sales producers in the advertising calendar industry lost his grip on the market because he listened to a discouraging story and let it affect his attitude. He had been told that "nobody wants calendars any more." Taking this seriously, he began to lose sales. A competing salesman heard the same story several times from probably the same reluctant prospects. This man, however, refused to accept the story as fact. Instead he surveyed the market and he learned that retail sales of calendars were up, indicating a public demand for them, but sales of advertising calendars had dropped off in some lines. This salesman made a change in pace and profited by it. He used the retail sales record on calendars as a selling tool. He went out and sold the idea that businessmen could profit by satisfying this demand and promoting their own businesses at the same time. He sold the idea that these businessmen could get their promotional messages posted on the walls of potential customers' living rooms, offices and public places at low unit cost by using calendars as a medium of sales promotion. Result: The latter salesman, by a change of pace and take-charge salesmanship, became a whiz at selling calendars. He accomplished this by positive action to counteract negative thinking—a constructive change in pace.

A heat wave slowed down a printing salesman. At 102 degrees it was too hot to stir up enthusiasm in his prospects. "Even the most attractive ideas in printing fell flat that day," this salesman said. "But, the heat suggested a profitable idea to me. It called for a change of pace. I switched to Christmas greeting cards on that torrid day and went after fuel dealer prospects. You see, Christmas was a cooling thought to bring to a discouraged fuel dealer in 102 degrees temperature. Heat has a depressing effect on a fuel dealer's business. I saw the attention value of Christmas cards when I dropped the sample book on my first prospect's desk. He looked at me and smiled as he wiped the perspiration from his bald head. He liked the idea of picking out Christmas cards in the heat. Perhaps it got his thoughts onto cold-weather prosperity for a fuel dealer. The switch in pace, however, paid off. He bought Christmas greeting cards, not only for his business, but for his personal use, too. I did a nice business in Christmas cards throughout that heat wave, by a switch in pace."

"It takes all sorts to make a world," according to an English proverb. This thought could well have been aimed at those of us who sell to keep the wheels of industry moving. The three-point principle of profiting by a change in pace in take-charge selling is this:

1. Know your people, their likes and dislikes; their needs and their wants.
2. Know your product and your market.
3. Innovate and be flexible.

CHAPTER SIX

HOW TO CONQUER SALES HAZARDS BY COMMAND SELLING

Case records provide ample evidence that a positive thrust can knock down obstacles which may threaten to set us back on our heels in selling. The positive thrust in selling is made up of three ingredients:

1. A unified selling plan, well conceived, well executed.
2. An attitude of bold selling with persuasive flexibility.
3. A self-motivating personal conviction that the product or service which we have for sale can benefit the buyer and that it can best be sold to him by us.

The initial step to get this trio into action for hazard-crushing power is to activate those ingredients by simply answering a few direct questions. First, what are we really up against? What are the hazards that give so many of us the jitters? What can we do to conquer those hazards?

Some of us may be inclined to wilt when we run up against what we think is a major hazard. This tendency, which we have now identified, may possibly be our most dangerous hazard. To combat this hazard let us find a dynamic, action-promoting substitute for it. Let us turn back to the mirror trick to which we have already been introduced. The mirror trick has demonstrated its merit in fortifying many would-be take-charge salesmen. For instance:

(a) The mirror trick has been the means of identifying major hazards which have plagued take-charge sales people. They have discovered that fears have been holding them back. By identifying this hazard they have learned how to conquer this hazard. The secret weapon: High-gear self-motivation.

(b) By using the mirror trick take-charge salesmen have identified certain sales-destroying bugaboos, such as price bugaboos, wrong time bugaboos, comparative value bugaboos, bad weather bugaboos and scores of others. They were familiar ghosts for those take-charge salesmen and by simply identifying those bugaboos those take-charge salesmen were able to present a bold front to those hazards and down them.

(c) The mirror trick convinced those take-charge salesmen that they were really fighting ghosts. Most of the hazards which they had conquered turned out to be ghostly creatures. For a time they haunted those sales people. The ghosts robbed them of selling power. They picked their pockets. By simply identifying those detructive ghosts those take-charge salesmen also discovered effective weapons to use against those ghosts. Among those weapons were these:

No. 1—Self-demanding self-mastery.

No. 2—Dynamic self-motivation.

No. 3—Increasingly persuasive power to provide the major thrust for take-charge salesmanship to conquer sales hazards and thereby increase total sales volume.

H. G. Wells left us an inspiring thought which applies to our struggle to conquer sales hazards. He said: "What on earth would a man do with himself if something did not stand in his way?"

A young man with a growing family lost his job as a catering manager in a private club. This man was what some call "down on his luck." Perhaps Ralph Waldo Emerson had someone in mind who resembled that catering manager when he wrote: "I am a great believer in luck. The harder I work the more of it I seem to have." That young catering manager who had been deprived of his job had been inspired by take-charge salesmen whom he had met in the club. Jobless, he applied for and secured a sales position in the janitorial supply division of a chemical firm. From the start he faced up to sales hazards. He knocked them down. He studied and worked hard. He prospected well. He planned his sales calls in advance. He built sales volume by bold selling. Necessity had motivated this man to succeed. He took dynamic action and profited by it. He continued to capitalize on "necessity" which the mirror trick had identified to him. But, he used "necessity" as a selling tool in selling janitorial supplies to plants and institutional prospects. He convinced purchasing agents that his products were necessary, that his products were beneficial to users, that they were desirable, and that they were good "buys."

That young man capitalized on optimism and on bold selling. He developed volume by patience and persistence. He conquered many sales hazards. Doing this, he enriched himself. He also became a benefactor in his own way to those he served. He became in fact a take-charge salesman.

SIMPLE RULES FOR MAINTAINING A TAKE-CHARGE SPIRIT

We see the results of applying the simple rules for maintaining a take-charge spirit by observing take-charge sales people hitting the volume-building trail. Door-bell-ringing sales people and party-plan sales people build sales volume by the take-charge spirit. In lieu of showing their wares to one housewife at a time, party-plan sales people go in for mass selling. In the living room of their "hostess" they display their wares to "invited guests." They build sales volume by introducing new ideas for the use of what they have to sell. They show their prospects how they can benefit by using what those take-charge sales people have to sell.

We see and hear take-charge sales people demonstrating their lines in the finest department stores. We meet them in business and professional clubs and in women's organization meetings. This is "captive audience" selling, but it requires take-charge salesmanship to make it productive. In all areas take-charge selling is on the march, doing a volume-selling job by supplying the simple rules of maintaining a take-charge spirit. Each of the following suggestions for maintaining a take-charge spirit has been tested, found to be practical, and proved to be productive:

    1. *IMPROVE MANAGEMENT TIME*—Take-charge salesmen profit by taking seriously what J. Willard Marriott,

business executive, said: "Time wasted now will haunt you all of your days, but taken advantage of, will build you a rich, successful and happy life."

2. *IMPROVE STRATEGY*—Plan calls better. Strengthen communication lines.
3. *DRAMATIZE*—Enliven sales presentations. Avoid dullness. Seize interest.
4. *LEARN THE ART OF CONVERSATION*—Talk about others. Keep the spotlight on the prospect.
5. *CULTIVATE THE ART OF LISTENING*—Hear what is said. Concentrate on it. Profit by it.
6. *WIDEN FRIENDSHIPS*—Be tactful. Strive to win confidence in others in what we have to sell and in us.
7. *TRIPLE SALES POWER*—(1) Cultivate the art of persuasion. (2) Generate enthusiasm. (3) Maintain an optimistic take-charge sales spirit.
8. *LOOK AHEAD*—Opportunity for increased sales lies in the future. Be objective. See those distant opportunities.
9. *CAN YOU IMAGINE THAT?*—Stimulate imagination. Plan and sell creatively.
10. *FIGHT FOR BUSINESS*—Down with sales hazards. Down with dullness. Dramatize presentations. Down with boredom. Move faster. Stimulate prospects to act—to buy. Value minutes. Save time. Think big. Sell boldly.

The take-charge sales manager of a national newspaper syndicate detected the spark of a take-charge spirit in one of his writers. Tactfully he suggested to the writer that he try moving over to the sales staff. The writer scoffed at the idea. The sales executive dropped the idea. Then one day, some time later, he called the writer in and said: "I'm in a tight spot. I have an appointment to meet the editor of the largest paper in your home town. I filled you in the other day on what I have done to land a contract with that fellow. Now I'm in a tight spot. I can't keep that appointment. As a personal favor will you go down there and wrap up that contract for me?" After attempting a few excuses the writer agreed to go. What was the sales strategy that won him over? Two selling points were involved: (a) An appeal to self-interest. By doing this errand and doing it well he would establish himself strongly with a top executive in the syndicate. (b) He was challenged. The sales manager had asked him to wrap up the contract. (c) More self-interest appeal: To do a favor for a friend.

That writer-turned-salesman did a great job. He wrapped up that contract. As a result he became enthusiastic about selling. The sales manager became enthusiastic about the take-charge salesman. And that take-charge salesman continued to write and also to sell, and shot his sales record to a high level by conquering an insidious sales hazard—lack of confidence in his own ability to influence others sales-wise.

A salesman specializing in such products as abrasive belts and allied products used by industry made this point in explaining his growth in sales volume: "When I organize my selling time I plan my calls on a time basis. I also plan my calls on the basis of why I am making the calls. What I am really doing in this is enlarging my territory. By getting everything on a time basis I am able to make four calls in the same area in the same length of time that formally resulted in only two calls. Moreover, the time-planned calls were generally more productive. I cut out waste of time and converted minutes into more sales."

By more time-conscious planning and more dramatic presentations a salesman in office equipment increased his volume by simply making more calls and making them more effectively. "This required thoughtful planning," he explained. "I put an end to procrastination. I made livelier sales pitches. I put the interest of those to whom I tried to sell ahead of everything else. I learned to detect the time-killer and how to get away from him and get on to a better prospect. It all adds up to holding a firm grip on sales planning and on sales presentations."

SIMPLE RULES FOR BUILDING PRODUCTIVE PUBLIC RELATIONS

When a take-charge salesman begins his day he is, in fact, heading into the market place with three missions in mind: (a) To make sales. (b) To build up his stature as a salesman. (c) To create good will for his firm and for the products or services which he sells.

Good will is an intangible asset. Often it has more substance in commerce than the appraised value of tangibles. Good will is the life blood of what we know as productive public relations. Take-charge salesmen personally profit by building productive public relations and by capitalizing on established and merited good will of the buying public.

One big producer in the communications field told a group of his fellow salesmen that the most disturbing thing he encounters in selling is to have a prospect say: "What's that? I've never heard of it." This productive salesman had put his finger on the heart of the public relations problem. Effective public relations creates an unforgettable image—a favorable reputation for a product, for a service, for a firm, or for an individual, which includes the take-charge salesman. That favorable image has high resale value, as the high-producing communications specialist can testify. To his colleagues he said this: "Don't cringe when someone tells you that you've been talked about favorably at a garden party. It's the lowest cost publicity you'll ever get and it may yield future sales for you."

A take-charge insurance salesman who specializes in big-ticket sales declared: "My greatest assist in writing the volume that is on my record is a reputation for being on the level. In every way I do try to be on the level. That isn't saintly. It's just good business. I try to keep the interests of my prospects and clients uppermost in any deal. I intend to continue along that road. That is a profitable road and yet it can be pitted with ruts. We are the losers if we violate the basic rules of productive public relations."

Another take-charge salesman writes volume orders in supplying industrial and institutional accounts with hardware and operating equipment. He attributes his success to rules which he has set up out of his own experience and which he adheres to. "These rules make up my personal sales doctrine," he said. "They have produced sales in volume for me. I suggest that every salesman set up his own set of rules and make them the topping for his knowledge of his product, his territory, and of those he serves or hopes to serve."

Here are six of that take-charge salesman's own simple rules for productive public relations:

1. Develop the right attitude toward work. Know your product. Develop a constructive attitude toward it, toward your firm, toward your territory, and toward those within that territory.
2. Bear in mind that you are always on display. Be exacting in personal conduct.
3. Deal fairly, even with competitors.

4. Advance the interests of customers. It's profitable.
5. Speak no evil. Show no prejudices. Be friendly. Praise your competitors. Praise the house you represent. Praise the community where your customers or prospective customers live and do business. Avoid religious and political squabbles.
6. Be sincere. Sincerity is a sales-builder.

Productive public relations go deep into the work of take-charge salesmen. It is good will on a broad basis. For instance, according to a perceptive sales executive in the construction industry, "fouled up" orders can put a salesman on the doubtful list. He rates care in writing orders as a good-will builder. His rule: Check the address. Be sure it is correct. Check the prices. Recheck unit prices and totals before you ask the buyer to sign. An error anywhere leaves a poor impression of the salesman. It may cause delay in shipment, conflict in billing, all of which may haunt the salesman. Good will is built by painstaking care in small details.

The operator of a chain of service stations discovered that the neatest shops in his chain usually ran up the highest totals in sales. This, of course, placed neatness up front as a factor in productive public relations. To this operator with the mind of a take-charge salesman it was evident that the public enjoys cleanliness, neatness, courtesy and a readiness to serve the buyer. And, he capitalized on this factor in productive public relations.

A new salesman in the office supply business promised a customer that he would find and have delivered to him a specified brand and quality of carbon paper. To keep his promise to that customer that take-charge salesman drove nearly a hundred miles to secure the much-wanted carbon paper and deliver it as promised. Worth it? After five years in the territory it appears that it was. He is the top producer in that area. Competition doesn't seem to disturb his steady upward sales record. He, too, operates on his own sales-building public relations rules and makes his operation profitable.

SIMPLE RULES FOR GENERATING ENTHUSIASM

I was striving to persuade a long-time client to change his promotion program. I sincerely believed that my idea would step up sales volume in his business. He was cool to my plan. Later I came up with a new angle for firing up his promotion program. This angle gave my basic idea broader scope and greater interest. This new angle got me so excited that I spent most of a sleepless night figuring out the possibilities in it for my client. Next morning I barged in on him. I was now all worked up about my idea with its new angles. I opened up on my client with a spirit of excitement I had never experienced before. This enthusiasm took hold of him, too. The result: We drafted a comprehensive promotion program from which both of us profited. The secret of the success of this about-face was simply a well-thought-out idea presented with enthusiasm.

Charles A. Schwab, the great industrialist, who had the capacity to "sell" his ideas, said this about enthusiasm: "A man can succeed at almost anything for which he has *unlimited enthusiasm.*" For take-charge salesmen unlimited enthusiasm is the magic element which often accounts for soaring sales records in many lines.

Two persons must become enthusiastic if that magical element is to attain its highest potential in sales productions. First, the salesman's enthusiasm must reach the excitement stage. Second, the prospective buyer, by being exposed to the excitement of the salesman, contracts the fever of enthusiasm and the inevitable result is a sale.

Consider the following three-way method of stirring up enthusiasm:

1. *SHOCK EFFECT*—Do something unusual, something appealing, something that crackles with action. Go after the immediate and favorable attention of the prospect.
2. *ACQUISITIVENESS*—Appeal to the self-interest of the prospect. Discover his sensitive area. Feed it. Generate enthusiasm for what your product or service can do for your prospect.
3. *HOW ENTHUSIASTIC CAN YOU GET?*—Unless we become excited about what we have to sell, what reason has the buyer to become excited? Unless we get hot it's a safe bet our prospects will remain cold. On the other hand, success comes to take-charge salesmen who act enthusiastic, who get excited about what they have to sell and dramatize the possibilities of their products or services, and who keep on hammering on that tender self-interest area of the prospect, until the contagion of enthusiasm generates buying fever in the prospect.

Samuel Goldwyn, the distinguished motion picture producer, had a long string of successes attributed to his ability to put across to others his ideas and his plans enthusiastically. "No person who is enthusiastic about his work has anything to fear from life," Goldwyn said.

I recall a young salesman who sold "spots" for radio commercials. While other salesmen were just getting by this young man was building sales volume. He seemed to have a fresh idea each morning on how his prospects could benefit from more liberal use of the commercial "spots" he sold. He showed excitement about his ideas. The result: Those who bought his ideas became enthusiastic and they talked about what a great idea that salesman had. The result: This take-charge salesman's enthusiasm wore off on his prospects and he profited along with them.

An insurance salesman broke away from an old concern which he felt had "gone to seed" and opened his own agency. A close friend asked him if he was quite sure everything would work out in his favor. The enthusiasm of the insurance salesman radiated from his sparkling eyes. "I'll make it happen my way," he assured his friend. And he did build a lucrative agency through his enthusiasm.

Walter P. Chrysler, who demonstrated how automobile sales could be made, contended that the secret of success in salesmanship is enthusiasm with excitement. "I like to see men get excited," Chrysler said. "When they get excited they get customers excited and we get business."

Requirements for generating enthusiasm: Interest, dedication, work and ginger. One salesman who listed and had demonstrated that he had those requirements scored big-ticket sales in commercial property development. He spoke to a group of salesmen representing a wide range of products. With the following thrust he stirred up their enthusiasm to conquer sales hazards of all kinds:

". . . How broad is your knowledge of your product? Show it. Get all wound up in it.

". . . What new ideas do you have that you believe will enable others to profit if they buy your product? List those ideas. Nurse those ideas. Go wild over those ideas. Then go out and sell those ideas.

". . . How enthusiastic are you about what you sell? Do you think you are offering a good deal? Then for heaven's sake show it.

". . . Can you get excited over anything that is good for you and good for others? Then show it and build sales volume by making that excitement contagious among prospective buyers."

SIMPLE RULES FOR CONTROLLING EXPENSES

A salesman, especially a take-charge salesman, concentrates each morning on the money he proposes to make out of increased sales volume in his allotted territory and in his allotted time. This attitude infuses his work with urgency. It sets up positive standards of value on the minutes and the hours which are his. To make those minutes and those hours yield maximum dividends for those of us who are in the take-charge selling class, we are required to recognize that by controlling our expenses we can contribute to our success. It is our method of controlling the costs of operation of our work.

To assist us in controlling expenses we have a few simple rules. These rules have been gleaned from experience records of scores of successful salesmen on the road. In applying those rules to our own operation there is great value in self-motivation, self-discipline, and attention to details. All this is related to solving the riddle of how to spiral sales volume upward to more profitable heights. Some of the simple rules which other take-charge salesmen have found helpful and profitable are these:

1. *WISE SPENDING*—Strive to make each outlay for business purposes increase our income. Look upon each expenditure as an investment. In this way we stress sales-building and its rewards, and submerge the expense and spending idea.

2. *WISDOM IN TRAVEL*—Cut down on mileage by more efficient consolidation of calls. Long, unprofitable miles overload operational costs. The rule: Plan calls in advance. Map calls in groups. Phone for appointments whenever possible and desirable. By saving mileage we save time.
   The principle: Invest in travel instead of overspending on it.

3. *WISDOM IN GOOD WILL SPENDING*—Expense accounts indicate that so-called "good will expenses" drain off substantial sums. Sound public relations effort can and does yield high returns in sales volume. However, good will spending requires more finesse than tossing loose change on a bar-room floor. It requires more than dating a cute chick and taking her to dinner in the swankiest club in town

merely because she is cute and holds down a job with a most desirable account on your prospect list. It may be doubtful whether she wields enough influence to swing any great volume of business to you. "Good will," as we know it in take-charge selling, is seldom open for bids. Seldom can it be purchased outright. It has to be earned. Good will is an intangible, challenging the best that is in us in tact and in skillful communication for persuasive selling.

4. *WISDOM IN CHOOSING OVER-NIGHT ADDRESSES*
   —When we arrive in a new town in which we plan to plow deeply for new business contacts, the question pops up: "Where do we stay for the night?" The answer calls for wisdom. We can spend or we can invest. We may save a few dollars by taking a low-cost room in a sub-standard motel or hotel. Those few dollars probably will yield nothing in the way of prestige or sales-building status for us. The alternative is to register at a well-rated motel or hotel. We might get more enjoyment out of the dining room in that well-rated establishment. There we might mingle with prospects whom we hope to make customers before another day passes. In that well-rated establishment we have a "good address." This gives us a certain amount of status in the business community. So, instead of the cost of over-night lodging being an expense we have made it an investment, which may have some influence in closing sales.

Samuel Johnson, the British author, left this tip which could apply to take-charge salesmen: "A man who both spends and saves money is the happiest man, because he has both enjoyments."

The comptroller for a large industrial concern spoke to a group at a regional conference of sales representatives. The substance of his message was this:

> I have noted some strange things in going over expense accounts. I have been impressed by the fact that some of our top producers spend less than low producers. You may wonder how this can be. All I can tell you is what I have learned from experience. I spent many years on the road. I was and I believe I still am a salesman. I learned that expenses ran higher on the days when I fell down on sales volume. . . . When I hit the ball the hardest my expenses dropped. From this I concluded

that one way to control my expenses while out in the territory
was to become so busy calling on prospects that I wouldn't have
time to think about anything else but selling. I am sure that
loose spending never assisted me in closing a sale. I am also sure
that you can't buy either good will or enduring sales volume.

SIMPLE RULES FOR KEEPING FIT

Dr. Paul Dudley White, famous heart specialist, has characterized
high blood pressure (hypertension) as the most important of ill-
nesses. This should give concern to take-charge salesmen and encourage them to follow the simple rules for keeping fit. Even Dr.
White's advice seems simple enough: "Avoid stress."

As take-charge salesmen we commit our physical and mental
resources to building "healthy" sales volume. Those in a position to
know assure us that our drive to succeed can be "healthy," that it
need not necessarily develop stress.

Here's the picture: Sales obstacles are "healthy" challenges to
take-charge salesmen. They summon their reserve power to crush
sales hazards. Those who keep fit commit their reserve power to
action without racing into a "killing" pace. One medical authority
defined stress as a product of emotional and intellectual power "gone
haywire."

We have previously been shown how to take command of selling
situations without abusing our bodies. We are advised by competent
authority to *invest* in care of our bodies. We are advised to conserve
our strength. We are advised to build up reserve power. We are also
advised to replenish reserve power when selling situations require
that we draw heavily on reserve power to attain a desirable objective.
Some medical authorities tell us that it is possible to become keyed
up, to become excited about a project, to become "healthily" enthusiastic without becoming tense. Can we then as take-charge salesmen get along with the following simple rules for keeping fit? The
stakes are high. Apply the following eight rules to you and to your
situations:

1. Go to a competent physician, in whom you have confidence,
   at least once a year, even oftener if you feel below par, and
   have a thorough physical examination.
2. Eat less. Choose a sensible, well-balanced diet. Tell your

doctor what you eat. It may be revealing to him and enable him to better advise you on keeping fit.

3. Keep weight down, to what your physician will tell you is within "clinical standards." When you try to reduce, get your doctor in on the program.
4. Drink less. We refer to alcoholic beverages. Total abstinence may be the best for you. Ask your doctor about it.
5. Smoke less. Total abstinence from tobacco may be of great benefit to you. Again the rule: Ask your doctor about your smoking habits.
6. Be kind to your heart. Consult your doctor and follow his advice on all matters affecting the heart.
7. Be kind to your digestive tract. Don't risk practicing medicine on yourself. Consult your doctor about stomach distress before gulping do-it-yourself remedies.
8. Work hard. Avoid stress. Play hard. Avoid stress. Eat regularly and moderately while relaxed. Get ample rest. Avoid taking your problems with you to bed or to the dining table. Laugh once in a while. It's a tension-freeing tonic.

A physician in general practice made this observation about keeping fit:

It would be profitable for many of my patients who are engaged in business to look at keeping fit as part of their investment program. Too many get the idea that keeping fit is something cooked up by doctors or exercise fanatics. I accused one of my patients of being more conscious of the welfare of his car than he was of his own body. I tried to convince him that the greatest asset he has in his business is his physical and mental well-being. I reminded him that if his car is slow starting in the morning he probably does something sensible about it. But, I asked him, if he is slow starting what does he do about that? I reminded him that if one of his office machines fails to function properly he calls for a specialist to fix it. I accused this man of doing much less for his body than he does for either his car or one of his office machines. The man to whom I was speaking had delayed a physical checkup too long. He had trouble which could have been headed off had he taken time out for a physical checkup in time. In my language as a doctor, that patient of mine was making several poor investments, although he was making money.

SIMPLE RULES FOR UNCOVERING SALES IDEAS FROM EVERY SITUATION

A hardware salesman ran up an amazing volume of sales in an area spotted by small towns and vast acres of wheat. This had been "poor territory" for other salesmen. Things changed, however, when a salesman we'll call Dave Norton took over. He had a home-spun idea about selling. It went like this: "It's sort o' like plowing ground," he said. "There's some soil that produces and some that won't. You never know until you plow into it."

Take-charge salesmen have plowed and uncovered sales ideas in many areas. Wherever people assemble alert take-charge salesmen can pick up ideas on which they can capitalize. For instance, a food products salesman made it a point to "drop in" on farm celebrations and auctions. "People who jammed those events knew all about good eating," this salesman said. "The women and the men would argue about what was the best and what was the worst brand on the market. A man selling food products, as I am, can hit pay dirt at these gatherings. I found out there what people want and I go out and capitalize on their wants and their needs. I encourage my dealers to buy from me to supply those wants and those needs."

A sales executive in the publishing industry said: "Uncovering sales ideas really is a form of prospecting. It's a method of skillfully stimulating potential buyers to reveal what they want, what they need, or what they think they need. With that done the salesman is fed a diet of fresh ideas from which he can create sales volume."

That same sales executive offered this tip: "A man in trouble often pours out a flood of ideas which salesmen who have learned to listen can turn into sales volume. Sales ideas exist in most situations. The more controversial the situation the more productive it can be. The more diversified a debate may turn out to be the richer it becomes in ideas."

Ideas do not fall into the laps of salesmen who make no effort to uncover ideas. Take-charge salesmen plow deeply in the soil of their territories for sales-producing ideas. There are tested ways by which take-charge salesmen have written high sales volume in previously low-producing territory. They have capitalized on ideas. The following simple rules have uncovered sales ideas in various sales situations:

1. *INVESTIGATE*—Broaden your knowledge of what you

sell, of its uses, and of the territory in which you propose to develop sales volume. Know your market and its people well.

2. *COMMUNICATE*—Converse with people. You never can tell who might be able to profit by using what you have to sell. Open the gates by conversation and listen to the ideas as they flood out for you to capitalize on.

3. *QUERY*—Expand communication by asking questions. Replies to your questions are often rich with ideas. Those ideas are your challenge to take charge of new selling situations.

4. *IMAGINE THAT*—Stimulate your creative power. Imagine how the man who has never bought your product could benefit by trying it. The possibilities are endless. For instance, you may sell carpet sweepers. Why should your prospect buy your sweeper and why should he (or she) buy it from you. Imagine that! It may mean a sale.

SOLVE PROBLEMS—Few gestures open the gates to more sales as well as a gesture of helpfulness. Offer a workable solution for a problem which has baffled your prospect and you will have created a selling situation so favorable that competition will have little possibility of getting a hearing.

When we have fortified ourselves with ideas which have been uncovered from various situations we then face the challenge of capitalizing on those ideas.

One eminent sales director told a sales conference what to do with new ideas. "Muster enough self-confidence to go out with your ideas and fight for business with a determination to close sales," he said, and then he added: "I found out in selling real estate, insurance and also in putting across my personal ideas that I had to strengthen my self-confidence. I had to get knowledge. I had to get experience. I had to banish from my mind the handicap of self-depreciation, timidity and fear. Experience taught me that sales resulted when I took charge of sales situations, when I knocked down sales hazards by bold selling."

SIMPLE RULES FOR CASHING IN ON TAKE-CHARGE SELLING

A friend of mine thumped the table and roared to a group of sales people who sold everything from needles to sports cars: "I feed and clothe my family by selling detergents," he said. "I do well at it because I believe I am doing a good thing for merchants who stock and promote my detergents and I believe I am doing something beneficial for those who buy those detergents from my merchant customers. It doesn't matter what we sell," he cried out to his eager-to-listen audience, "just so we sell it on a clean-cut basis of benefitting the guy who buys it. Some of you may snicker and say that I can't pile up sales volume with a cleaning product, but I have proved that it can be done. I see dramatic possibilities in suds bubbling in an automatic washer. Those suds make me happy. I believe that women who buy my stuff have more delightful wash days than those who don't. They enjoy greater pride in their clean clothes just because they used my detergent. All that isn't puff. We have to have faith and pride in what we sell. It's the gentleman's view of this game we call selling. You can profit by being gentlemen-salesmen. It will give you an edge on brash competitors. At times it requires guts to be a gentleman in a tight, no-holds-barred selling situation, but it pays off."

The distinguished author, John Galsworthy, who wrote *The Forsyth Saga, The Skin Game* and other novels, took an interesting slant on being a gentleman. It is recommended as good before-breakfast reading for take-charge salesmen. Galsworthy wrote: "A man asked to define the essential characteristics of a gentleman—using the term in its widest sense—would presumably reply, 'The will to put himself in the place of others; the horror of forcing others into positions from which he would himself recoil; the power to do what seems to him to be right, without considering what others may say or think.'"

Did not Mr. Galsworthy expose in those few words a refined form of persuasion which has profited many masters of the selling art?

The objective of each step in take-charge salesmanship is to cash in on the art of persuasion in bold selling. The first step in attaining this objective in any selling situation is to crush any sales hazard which threatens to block our progress.

At a dinner honoring a building supply salesman who had moved into big-figure sales by volume-selling in everything from nails to nuts and bolts and from prefabricated cabins to carload shipments of lumber, this take-charge salesman was asked how he did it. In his quiet way he replied: "I treat 'em decent, give 'em lots of fresh ideas to saw and hammer on, and show 'em how to best use what I have to sell. I try to do all this in a way that they will believe they can do it and make money at it. I find that if I can do that sales just naturally pile up for me."

From case records of the achievements of take-charge salesmen we learn that certain rules govern the art of developing sales in volume. There are rules also for tearing down sales barriers, for crushing sales hazards and for cashing in on bold take-charge selling. Here are some of those simple rules:

1. *AROUSE INTEREST*—A dental supply salesman declares that he gets the immediate attention of dentists by presenting endorsements of his products and laboratory reports of their quality, and by talking to the dentists about how his products have proved their worth in enabling dentists to do a better professional job. All of this ties in with self-interest appeal.

2. *SELF-MOTIVATION*—A salesman handling outdoor sports equipment nudges himself into action in this way: "I study my line, talk about it a lot and examine and reexamine my line myself. All this gets me excited about my line and, so, I go out to get others excited about it."

3. *BACK UP THAT STATEMENT*—If we make a claim for what we have to sell we increase the selling power of the claim by supporting it with solid evidence. Case records showing how others profited or otherwise benefited by using what we have to sell has great selling power.

4. *IDEAS WITH SALES PUNCH*—A salesman in residential park development property cashes in on listening. "I listen to complaints as well as to compliments. Both may be loaded with selling ideas from which I can profit."

5. *CULTIVATE GOOD WILL*—The **principle:** Sincerity, honesty, square dealing and unselfish service have paid off by contributing to volume sales for take-charge salesmen. These virtues seem to enable take-charge salesmen to be more fully armed to combat sales hazards and do a better selling job.

CHAPTER SEVEN

HOW TO COMMAND THE PAPER WORK AND NOT VICE VERSA

A sales executive of a western paper products outlet taught his sales force how to avoid getting tangled up in excessive paperwork. His doctrine: Excesses in paperwork are due to three foes of productive salesmanship:

(a) Lack of clear thinking.
(b) Lack of constructive planning.
(c) Lack of time-management.

Our military services are often accused of being masters of the art of developing paperwork into a major project. The soldier calls this "red tape." Moreover, the soldier isn't "sold on the idea," and this fact makes this sort of productivity in paperwork pertinent in selling. As one filing clerk remarked: "When we dump the contents of these filing cases on our prospective customers they'll have to buy or smother."

An authoritative definition of red tape is "rigid office procedure involving *delay* or *inaction.*" With that in mind we are, as take-charge salesmen, challenged to take action. Anything which holds up the selling process or encourages inaction calls for positive counter-action. Within this situation we also have this warning for take-charge salesmen:

Take command of paperwork or paperwork will take command of you.

A jewelry salesman who has a record of steady growth in sales volume explained how he handles paperwork and makes it profitable:

> One small box is my total record file when I am on the road.
> I hold paperwork down to fit that small filing case. Unless I do
> this, paperwork threatens to bury me. Should this happen I
> would have to dig out from under the deluge in order to get on
> with the job of selling jewelry. It is by selling jewelry that I
> make money. I try to make paperwork contribute to this. My
> small filing case, carried with me in my car, compels me to
> evaluate everything that comes to me in the mail and also that
> which I am tempted to store away. With only one small case
> as a storage vault in and out of my working area in my home
> I am compelled to squeeze all my paperwork into a single and,
> yet, simple mold: *NECESSITY.*

We have among salesmen and sales executives those who think in terms of paperwork. Habitually they attempt to convert the simplest sales problems to paper. The result is a flow of memoranda from the paperwork enthusiasts in the field to the home office, and from the paperwork enthusiasts in the home office to the sales force in the field. Were sales always on the uptrend to keep pace with that flood of paperwork all of it would be justified. However, too often the record usually indicates the opposite is the result. Here is the danger point:

When paperwork takes charge of a salesman it enslaves him, cuts into sales volume, reduces income.

Five ways for take-charge salesmen to combat the threat of excessive paperwork:

1. Take command of the situation.
2. Reduce paperwork to productive essentials.
3. Make paperwork a selling tool.
4. Employ paperwork as a time-saver.
5. Employ paperwork to maintain a check on your own progress.

HOW TO PROFIT BY PAPERWORK:

(a) Simplify record-keeping.
(b) Learn and practice the art of brevity. Write informal memos in lieu of long-winded epistles. Make a simple "O.K." serve the purpose of a formal letter whenever possible and appropriate.
(c) Simplify your filing system. Make a card file do the work of an expansive filing case in many instances, thereby reducing the necessity of searching through stacks of documents for information which can be briefed and indexed on a card.

Take-charge salesmen can profit by rereading the suggestion once made by Nelson A. Rockefeller: "To extol extremism whether in 'defense of liberty' or in 'pursuit of justice' is dangerous, irresponsible and frightening."

Of course, Mr. Rockefeller was not talking specifically about salesmanship when he made that statement but the import of what he said has a definite bearing on take-charge salesmen combatting extremism in paperwork.

The principle: To be a take-charge salesman take command of paperwork. Rebel against paperwork enslaving you. Find ways to use paperwork as a tool in take-charge selling. Dig deeply into your files. In those "dead" records there may be hidden sales ideas from which you can profit.

SIMPLE RULES FOR EFFICIENTLY HANDLING PAPERWORK

An efficiency consultant once remarked: "The easiest thing for any of us to do is to start something that will mess things up." He was discussing the tendency to overdo paperwork. He pointed out that take-charge salesmanship requires that a salesman take command of every aspect of paperwork. "Paperwork, when related to selling, requires systematic operation," the analyst declared. "It requires a plan that is free of 'bugs'. It requires a method of operation that contributes to selling and does not ever hinder it."

Paperwork is particularly vulnerable to complexity. Take-charge salesmen get ahead by mastering that "bug" in paperwork. They simplify their paperwork. From the records of many take-charge salesmen we discover that paperwork and its problems are common with most of them. From those same records we have extracted some of the simple rules which have enabled those take-charge salesmen to oust paperwork from a command position and have enabled them to take command of the situation themselves. Here are five of those pertinent rules:

1. Take pride in brevity. Reduce each memo, each letter, each informal note to the fewest words required to effectively convey your message. Be specific.

2. Evaluate before committing any document to the files. Stop, read, understand. Under pressure the tendency is to stuff into the file anything that doesn't cry out for immediate attention. This leads to files becoming dumping grounds. Ask yourself: Should this be kept? Why? Should it be acted on now? Why? What action does it require?

   The principle: Do something about it instead of brushing it off your desk or hiding it away in a file.

3. Turn filing cards into sales and profits. Four by six inch cards are most convenient and are large enough for most messages. Such cards often become nuggets of sales producing ideas. Take-charge salesmen profit by keeping them current. They go over their cards frequently. They keep them "alive." Take-charge salesmen find such cards easy to carry with them, in their pockets, in a brief case, and handy to have in a desk drawer. They are space-savers, time-savers, and, when made the most of, become, in fact, nuggets of sales-producing ideas.

4. Set up a work system fitted to your personality and to your "M.O."—method of operation. Lay a heavy hand on any tendency to carry paperwork to the extreme. Keep it within the bounds of profitable efficiency. Measure your system by its sales-producing efficiency. Strive to convert paperwork into a selling tool. When an idea involving paperwork pops into your mind pin it down with such questions as these: Will this idea increase paperwork? If it does, will this be justified by its effect on sales? Or, will this idea become a new time-consuming project which will slow me down and turn out to be a retardant to my selling power? Keep paperwork on the positive, sales-producing side.

5. Enrich your files with sales ideas. Clean out deadwood frequently. Know what data you have on file. Know where you can get at it quickly. Keep it at your finger tips. Evaluate

every idea for its sales possibilities. Get those fertile ideas out of their hiding places in glutted files. Convert them into sales.

An unusually busy insurance salesman amazed many of his colleagues by his command of the paperwork problem. This was his secret: "My system boils down to three essentials: *DO IT NOW. DO IT EFFECTIVELY. DO NOT PROCRASTINATE.*"

This take-charge salesman further explained his system:

> Procrastination can mean only one thing in getting paperwork out of the way. It will accumulate paperwork in another place. To master this problem requires decision after decision. I devote time each evening at home, or if I am on the road, in a hotel room, to get my correspondence and reports out of the way. I fight against letting paperwork pile up. It can become a mountainous monster. I tackle paperwork instead of avoiding it.

That insurance specialist obviously has devised a system suitable to his personality and to his method of operation. The combination has become profitable for him. It was Victor Hugo who wrote: "He who plans the transactions of the day, and follows out that plan, carries a thread that will guide him through the labyrinth of the most busy life."

HOW TO PROFIT BY WRITING NOTES TO YOURSELF

Writing notes to yourself can become a sound and profitable habit. One take-charge salesman who profited by writing notes to himself described it as "creative scribbling." He said:

> I write notes to myself for two reasons: First, I am addicted to note-writing. Then it is a protective device for me. I distrust my memory. If a big sale is at stake I lack complete faith in my memory. So, I scribble what I believe I must remember. I make notes of bits of information which might become vital in closing the sale. As I make my rounds I learn about things that can be turned into sales power, so I jot those things down. My notes include things I have overheard, things I have been told, or just fleeting thoughts of how I might land a piece of business.

Most people who profit by writing notes to themselves are what I choose to call "note-writing addicts." They are hooked by the habit and it is profitable for them. Horace Mann said: "Habit is a cable. We weave a thread of it every day, and at last we cannot break it."

A take-charge salesman who represented one of the nationally known bedding manufacturers told a group of his colleagues that he traced many of his best sales to self-directed note-writing. "I recommend that you get hooked by this habit as I did," he said. That salesman was typical of those who use note-writing as a sales tool. John Jacob Astor, who had a speaking acquaintanceship with wealth, supported the profit possibilities of constructive habits, of which note-writing is one. Wealth, said Mr. Astor, is largely a matter of habit. The bedding salesman declared that Astor's viewpoint on the worth of good habits "grabbed" him, and, as a result, he became a note-writing addict and profited by it.

As a back-up for a fickle memory the habit of writing notes to yourself can be made a profitable selling tool. It can become a reliable memory-jogger. It can save you from failing to keep important appointments.

As a creative habit writing notes to yourself has the power to generate a flow of fresh ideas. Those ideas can be turned into personal profit by providing fuel for enthusiastic take-charge salesmanship.

The possibilities for sales and profit in note scribbling are indicated in the following instances:

. . . The name of a prospect you had never thought of before.

. . . Flash ideas on how you can do more productive prospecting.

. . . Better ways to classify prospects for developing greater sales volume.

. . . Character slants on prospective buyers. Things you have found out about those prospects, about their accomplishments, about their personalities, about their ideals, their hobbies, their ambitions. Jot down all you can find out about prospective buyers and use those notes as selling tools.

. . . A hint from a housewife, a hostess, or from a secretary of how she made productive use of your product or a similar product.

. . . A tip on a new aggressive campaign being contemplated by your most challenging sales competitor.

. . . A tip on why a competitor lost out in his bid for a big chunk of business in which you are interested.

. . . A tip on how and why a salesman in your line, or in some related line, succeeded in closing sales in volume.

. . . A reminder that you have an appointment with Mr. Good Prospect at 2 p.m., together with a few notes about this prospect which might prove valuable to you in persuading this prospect to buy what you have to sell.

. . . A personal observation about a new community development and how and why it might have sales possibilities for you.

. . . A reminder to do your paperwork in off hours thus enabling you to tear yourself away from the ease of your swivel chair and the personal appeal of your executive-type desk, for sales are developed in the field in person-to-person persuasive contacts with prospective buyers and not by meditating in an office sanctuary.

Profits from writing notes to yourself result from getting thoroughly hooked by the habit. It is then that results become cumulative. Of course, there are good and bad habits. Worry is a destructive habit, sales-wise. Note-writing is a positive, constructive, stimulating and creative habit. Enthuiastic take-charge sales people profit by this habit. One authority states that when we memorize something we forget as much of it in the first eight hours as during the next three weeks. This seems to support the idea that writing notes to ourselves is a constructive habit with great sales potential.

Should you be confronted with a challenging sales problem one authority on the subject suggests: "Sweep your desk clear of paperwork and write a note to yourself. By writing that note you will crowd worry into the background and generate constructive thinking about sound solutions for your problem."

Note these five guidelines for note-writing to yourself, which is a form of paperwork that can be made productive:

1. If a sales problem worries you, make notes defining the problem.
2. Identify, by notes, what created the problem.
3. List all possible solutions of the problem.
4. Choose the best solution, develop it in writing, and then attack the problem with the zest of a take-charge salesman.
5. Profit by writing an explanatory note to yourself on how you solved or failed to solve that sales problem and the reasons for your success or failure. This note will become a valuable sales tool when similar problems occur.

HOW TO GET THE TOP VALUE OUT OF BEING KEYED UP

We have just considered productive habits. Related to such habits is how to get keyed up and make it pay.

Excitement is the key to enthusiasm. To be keyed up is to be excited, to be enthusiastic. The objective in getting keyed up, for take-charge salesmen, is to capitalize on it by increasing sales volume. That may seem too obvious but to be keyed up involves attitude, self-discipline, self-management, courage, creativity, imagination and the joy we get out of constructive effort. Those are the qualities we find in take-charge salesmen. The take-charge salesmen who become keyed up release their persuasive energy by becoming excited over what they sell. They capitalize on their own enthusiasm. They get their enthusiasm out in the open. They do not hide it. They show that they are keyed up. Result: More sales, greater pride in achievement for the salesman—top value for them. They became keyed up and they knew how to make the most of it.

Exciting moments come to take-charge salesmen in various phases of their work. They scan routine reports with imaginative zeal. They appraise future appointments and plan to follow through with fire in their presentations. Imaginative sales people detect in their appointment books opportunities for sales and this keys them up. They come across a reminder of a past incident. This keys them up. They react to such reminders with renewed eagerness to go back over the trail and cash in on what may have been a missed opportunity. In this attitude there is expectancy, which, too, keys them up.

A take-charge salesman specializing in investment securities said:

> It is exciting to meditate on plans, on hopes, on possibilities and how I can convince a prospect that he can achieve his goal in business or in life in general. A few minutes of that sort of musing often gives birth to new ideas for me. I get all keyed up and this stimulation hangs on as I go out to tackle my next prospect. This sort of excitement is a contagious thing but my records show that it holds the secret of solid sales progress.

The advertising and sales club was an exciting place that afternoon. One of its members, a take-charge salesman who bore the title of "account executive" in an advertising agency, had moved in on a much-sought-after account and the word had gotten around. In the face of tough competition he had come out of the tussle with a signed contract in his brief case. How did he capture this choice account? His boss explained it this way:

> He got keyed up on that deal some time ago. He has been living with it. He stuffed himself with know-how about that account's business and their method of operation. He went in to get that account loaded down with a whole package of fresh ideas for future campaigns. He had sold himself on each of the campaigns he was going to propose to that account. When he let go of all that pent up energy the executive board caught that salesman's spirit. They were captured by his sureness. He was convincing. He drew mental pictures for them of how market expansion and greater sales volume was within their reach. He stirred up those board members until they were competing with him for enthusiasm. He had them as keyed up as he was. Result: The board bought the whole package.

Take-charge salesmen condition themselves to getting keyed up. They are stimulated by reports of new products coming on the market. In those new products they see possibilities for added sales volume. These salesmen get keyed up making plans. Some take-charge salesmen get keyed up over simple things, such as simplifying their own method of controlling expenses while on the road or a method of keeping their tax records current.

The sales director for a broadcasting station made this observation to his staff: "We are finding out from your performance that there are two kinds of short cuts in salesmanship: (a) the short cut that falls flat, and (b) the short cut that gets you on the target on time and results in a sale. We are all vitally concerned with short cuts that result in more sales. I have seen short cuts which keyed up salesmen so they brought in new sales, all because they had the vision to detect sales possibilities in those short cuts."

Two neighbors, both salesmen, are interesting opposites. Salesman "A" heads for work in the morning with a cheerful attitude. He radiates enthusiasm as he waves to his wife and the kids and drives away for another day in the market place. He returns at night, still keyed up, and the kids run to greet him. He's that kind of guy. He gets keyed up about his home life, his work, and about life in general. He's enthusiastic about an evening of entertainment. It may be at home or it may be a night out. He goes at it with a spirit of excitement. His sales volume keeps going up. There is a reason for this.

He's a take-charge salesman who knows how to get keyed up and capitalize on enthusiasm.

Salesman "B", who lives next door to salesman "A," leaves home in the morning with no fanfare. He is a serious, thoughtful, matter-of-fact salesman. A major explosion is required to excite him. His sales presentations are solid, factual, but lifeless. They lack the zip and fervor which carry salesman "A's" presentations to the closing point.

Salesman "B", a solid citizen, rates lower in total sales than salesman "A". He closes fewer sales. He opens fewer new accounts than does salesman "A". The apparent reason for this achievement gap between these two neighbors is that one is colorful while the other lacks lustre. It may also be due to one being enthusiastic and the other lacking in enthusiasm. One gets keyed up and the other doesn't. Their records tell the story. The keyed-up salesman enjoys the big slice of the sales pie.

The speaker at a sales banquet honoring top producers made this significant statement: "This is a great crowd. Everybody is keyed up. We are here to throw earned bouquets to those who are always keyed up in their work. They get that way because they enjoy what they are doing and believe in what they are selling. In her book, 'Wake Up and Live,' Dorothea Brande wrote, 'it takes energy to fail.' Well, the sales people we are recognizing tonight for achievement refuse to waste their energy on failing. These men get keyed up to win and their excitement keys up others to buy from them."

HOW TO FIND LIVE SALES TIPS IN DEAD REPORTS

"That gives me an idea!"

Therein lies the possibility of increasing sales volume by following up tips unearthed from what we lightly refer to as dead reports.

Profitable excitement may often be found by exploring a variety of areas. Take-charge salesmen have exposed live sales tips, followed them up and developed them into sales volume, by purposeful reading in areas such as these:

. . . Industrial reports of new developments, relative sales gains and losses, price fluctuations, seasonal demands, regional sales trends, etc.

. . . Classified ads in daily newspapers published in the territory covered by take-charge salesmen. Help wanted ads may be indicative of activity in construction, industrial expansion, merchandising activity, etc.

. . . Chambers of Commerce reports of new business establishments, of new commercial, professional and social activity, of new home construction, etc.

. . . Taxpayer association reports showing trends of taxation and how it is or may affect the lines in which you are interested as a take-charge salesman.

. . . Public records of real estate sales, of building permits, of suits filed, any of which may affect the products which you sell. Even births and deaths may have some effect on your market.

. . . Case records to which you have access may show how notable sales have been made and may give you a clue to how to land additional business.

. . . Promotion literature of various types often reflects market activity and trends, and may provide tips for capitalizing on the information through imaginative take-charge salesmanship.

Purposeful reading of so-called dead reports can often get the wheels of imagination into motion. Limitless opportunities exist for take-charge salesmen who strive to keep ahead of the sales parade. They can gain useful knowledge of people, of products, of territory and of wants and needs. They can capitalize on all of this by purposeful reading to supplement experience and then by imaginative exploitation.

A salesman who specialized in commercial development properties once said: "My most thrilling reading is delinquent tax listings." Some of his colleagues called that remark the laugh of the day. But, that salesman had stated a fact. He had built a reputation for getting factories built on property which others had ignored. One case in point was some abandoned acreage which showed up on delinquent tax sale listings. The location of this property keyed up this take-charge salesman. He saw possibilities of hooking that property up to another of his listings. This would meet acreage requirements of a manufacturer of whom the salesman had knowledge. Much of that knowledge had been gained by reading "dead" reports. He brought the delinquent tax property to the attention of the manufacturer and convinced him of the possibilities by adding it to the adjacent property which the salesman had listed for sale. Moreover, this idea had dual benefits for this salesman. (a) It resulted in a substantial sale.

(b) It increased his stature in the eyes of the manufacturer and he became virtually a consultant on such developments for that manufacturer.

At the top of the list in paperwork requirements is purposeful reading. Many take-charge salesmen make their reading time the most productive period of the day. Their secret: Reading with a purpose to stimulate creative planning.

A toy salesman told a group of his fellow salesmen that he once considered his own sales-and-call reports to be deadly to review. He changed his attitude after this experience: "Just for kicks I picked up a batch of my old sales call reports," he said, "and went through them with an inquisitive mind. This paid off well. In those reports, which I had considered to be dead, I plucked out several live sales tips which resulted in substantial volume for me. After that I placed purposeful reading at the top of my paperwork chores."

An insurance salesman, educated and trained as a statistician, enjoyed poking fun at statistical reports when he detected inconsistencies in them. He changed his whole attitude toward reports when sales thoughts began coming to the surface in his mind. "In statistics I have found facts which even the most stubborn prospects could not refute," he said. "I mix those facts with ideas for benefitting my prospects. In that way I have converted reading time into profit-making time. I have also found similar opportunities in other phases of my paperwork. To find those live sales tips I had to change my attitude toward necessary paperwork."

HOW TO FIND EXTRA SALES-PRODUCING OPPORTUNITIES EVERY DAY

Inquisitive sales executives and inquisitive salesmen have been known to uncover sales-producing opportunities in reports of sales which have already been closed.

An inquisitive accountant in an office supply establishment changed the objectives of selling in that establishment. After checking over a stack of incoming orders he asked: "Why doesn't Jim sell this pet account of his on carload buying instead of writing all these dribbling orders?" The idea keyed up the sales manager. He discussed the problem with the accountant, who saw the possibility of savings for the buyer and overall margins favorable to the distributor. The sales manager saw the big picture of greater sales volume.

The result: New sales targets were set up for the sales staff to shoot at. They were taught to think big. Business in volume became the objective.

One salesman on the staff who abhorred paperwork cracked: "This should cut down on paperwork, or am I wrong?" He was wrong. Paperwork initiated the project which was producing sales volume and paperwork held on in that establishment. It became more important to thoughtful take-charge salesmen than a chore to complain about. It became a source of sales ideas—a tool in selling.

Paperwork in one form or another is involved in virtually every search for extra sales-producing opportunities. This sort of paperwork becomes exciting and profitable. Salesmen who get the most out of it remain in command of the paperwork. For instance, look at the following three areas in which paperwork can be made a source of sales opportunities and how it can be made profitable:

1. *BE MORE REALISTIC* and more enthusiastic about goal-setting.
2. *BECOME MORE VIGOROUS* and more resourceful about prospecting.
3. *BECOME MORE PERSUASIVE* in letter-writing, aiming at potential increases in sales volume as a by-product of constructive public relations.

A specialty salesman who covered a three-state territory sold executive gifts to a wide clientele. He maintained a record of satisfactory volume but he was dissatisfied. Marking time irked this man. He wanted to be on the move, ahead. So he set up new objectives to push his sales higher. He put all this down on paper. He wanted his own commitments to confront him and to challenge him.

First he wrote: "I will open one new account every week from now on." He was realistic about this. The challenge was to look for new sales opportunities. He searched for accounts that had stability and the potential for growth. After a few months in this self-assigned campaign this salesman became excited about his progress, so he increased the challenge. He doubled his objective. Now, he said, I will open two new accounts a week. A few years later this salesman was opening three accounts and then it went on to four and sometimes higher. That salesman had demonstrated the sales-producing value of taking command of paperwork, of setting up challenging objectives, of planning resourcefully and constructively.

A printing salesman convinced himself that a lot of people in his territory were not using printed stationery who could profitably do so. The thought excited him. He initiated a search for hidden sales possibilities. This was top-level prospecting. It entailed paperwork and it required that he take command of the paperwork. He launched his campaign by:

1. Assembling club membership rosters and identifying members by occupation. To do this he had to take command of an ambitious program of paperwork with unlimited sales possibilities. Result: A growing prospect list and fresh daily challenges for take-charge salesmanship.

2. Budgeting definite hours daily in which to screen listings in the telephone yellow pages. This, too, was paperwork, but that salesman maintained his enthusiasm. He was sold on his own idea.

3. Writing more letters with the warmth of sincerity in them. This required more purposeful reading and more purposeful listening. He discovered that letters of thanks for a courtesy had long-standing selling power. The same was true of letters of congratulation, complimentary letters, and letters of consideration for a prospect who becomes ill or who has suffered some misfortune.

Prospecting in its various forms requires paperwork. The trick is to make paperwork productive, to take command of it, to make it produce sales. By following through on the simple rules of handling paperwork efficiently, and by taking command of it as we take command of selling situations, we make paperwork a productive selling tool.

HOW TO BOOST YOUR SALES VOLUME AND YOUR PERSONAL STATUS BY TENSION-FREE TAKE-CHARGE SELLING

A representative of a top-rated home-study school visited a canning plant one day as the guest of the management. It was pay day. He observed men and women coming to the pay windows for their checks. Imaginative wheels turned over in that take-charge salesman's head. "Look at those hundreds of prospects," he thought. "This is a jackpot. I'll show those people how they can increase their incomes, how they can gain prestige, how they can realize their ambitions. Doing that I can make students out of them. If I can enroll just 10 percent of that crowd I'll have it made and I'll be doing something constructive for them."

That was the thinking of that take-charge salesman. He told me about that experience and what he eventually realized out of it. He boosted his sales volume beyond what he had first anticipated to be possible by enrolling cannery working people in correspondence study courses. But he did convince those men and women that they had it within themselves to "be somebody." He described his sales approach in this way:

He chose the most likely prospects out of the crowd and concentrated on them. He learned about them, about their personal lives, about their family lives by winning their confidence. He learned about their frustrations and some of their problems. The more intimate he became with these people the more he came to know what they would like to do with their lives. All of this was ammunition for take-charge salesmanship. He motivated them to commit themselves to study. He accomplished this by tension-free salesmanship.

A few hours spent in observation in a canning factory had opened the doors of opportunity for that take-charge salesman. He capitalized on those hours. He lifted himself up by benefitting those who yielded to his persuasive sales influence.

The secret of that salesman's success was not how he made a quick buck out of a one-day tour of a cannery. The secret was best explained by him: "I believe that I have to learn to see in order to sell," he said. "I have to learn to listen to people and to feel with them. I believe there are people everywhere who might become buyers of what I have to sell. Too many of us in selling fail to sell to our capacity because we are up tight. I believe that we must let down and expose our human side. We must have vision and feeling to sell. I need to look at and listen to people. I need to put myself in the place of my prospects in order to communicate effectively with them."

According to one successful sales-training director the job of boosting sales is a clear-cut challenge for us to "get going." It's a command for action, he said. He stressed that successful take-charge salesmen get rid of tension before they tackle a challenging prospect. He maintained that excitement and enthusiastically generated selling power have great potentials. "Conversely," he said, "when we tighten up and become tense, our prospects become tense. Mutual tension winds up with chilliness or even with excessive heat. This is a definite sales hazard. If we would sell to greater capacity, we need to get excited, we need to become enthusiastic, and we need to free ourselves of tension. We need to loosen up."

Boosting sales and raising personal status with buyers are closely related to success in selling. George Romney, automobile salesman with a dynamic record in this field, and also a persuasive politician, once said: "A measurement of success is whether you are doing the best you can." J. C. Penney left this encouraging thought: "Success in life does not depend on genius."

CHAPTER EIGHT

HOW TO MAKE TIME WORK
FOR YOU IN SELLING

Minutes are slippery. They can, however, become profitable to us in selling. We can manage them, work them. Those slippery minutes add up to our most valuable asset in selling.

While we in selling admit that time is valuable we do occasionally complain: "I don't have time for that or anything like it." But, even in this we admit that time has value. We also recognize the value of time when we harness minutes and hours and make them fully productive for us.

Time management is the answer to the problem of putting time to work for us and thereby enabling us to be more successful as take-charge salesmen. A highly productive representative of a chemical supply house used time management to create stability and progress for himself in selling. By managing the minutes and the hours allotted to him he won recognition in business circles. He became a dynamic leader in civic affairs, which opened doors of opportunity for him in selling. He "belonged." He got things moving ahead, including his own sales production. His associates dubbed him, "the spark plug." But, all this required time. For his use he had the same amount of time allotted to him as you and I have—24 hours a day. He made his allotted time work for him. He squeezed capacity performance out of each minute and out of each hour. He did this in this way:

He budgeted time as you and I must do if we intend to make the most of it. Time-budgeting is relatively simple and yet it can become highly productive for take-charge salesmen. It amounts to this:

(a) *ALLOCATE* a portion of your time for selling and related activity. Give this top priority. This is your source of income, your bread-and-butter project.

(b) *ALLOCATE TIME* for self-improvement. Success of your bread-and-butter project relies heavily on constant self-improvement. Study requires time.

(c) *PROVIDE TIME* for relaxation. Don Herald, artist and writer, suggested: "Slow down the muscles and stir up the mind." Salesmen on the road are inclined to tighten up to *catch* a jet flight, to *grab* something to eat, to *pursue* diversion. Relax! It's time to refuel!

(d) *SET ASIDE TIME* for tightening ties with your family. Your wife and your kids are closely allied to your top priority project—selling. Who else can motivate you more than they?

(e) *SACRIFICE SOMETHING* to find time for civic activities. Make your town a good town to live in and to sell in.

(f) *RESERVE TIME* for worship and church activity.

(g) *CALL TIME ON WORK* to provide time for keeping fit, time to rest, time to exercise, time to refresh mind and body, in order to be alert for another day in take-charge selling.

There we have seven spots out of the day and all require time. You may have some additions to make to the foregoing spots. Your situation and your working methods may differ from mine but neither of us can escape the fact that the elusive minutes which have been allotted to us are potent factors in our success plans. We have 24 non-elastic hours placed at our disposal to make the most of. We may divide these to our own advantage or to our detriment. The seven areas which have been suggested as time-consumers work out to less than 3½ hours for each of those areas. Obviously something must "give." Obviously we must innovate, we must "make" time if we would produce more in sales.

How to make time work for us in selling obviously is very much up to us individually. There is this surety about it: We must so budget our time that it will work for us. We must harness it so that minutes and the hours will become productive. Time management becomes our major daily challenge in take-charge selling.

HOW TO CULTIVATE A SENSE OF TIMING IN COMMAND SELLING

I learned something about the value of a sense of timing in Reno, Nev. I discovered that habits and timing have something in common. My well-chosen and well-classified prospects were business executives. In trying to contact these prospects I ran up against a familiar barrier. The secretaries would say: "I'm sorry, he's out of the office. He won't be back today." I made the rounds again the next day. Again my prospects were out. It was mid-summer and it was hot. I was losing time. At lunch time I sought refuge in the coolness of a downtown club. Several of the prospects I had were there. A few of them were noon-time napping in a basement slumber room provided for T.B.M's—tired business men. Next day I struck out earlier. I drove to the suburban office of one prospect I had seen in the club. It was 7 a.m. and he was at work. He invited me into his office. We got right down to business. I closed a sale. I told him that I had called before but had missed him. "Too late in the day," he replied with a smile. "Several of us have found out that we get more accomplished by getting to work early and knocking off early. In this way we get time to do a lot of community chores and mixing with others. This has proved profitable to us in our various lines." A sense of timing had enabled me to solve the problem of other men's habits, adjusting to them and thereby developing sales. My predecessors in that territory hadn't made those necessary early-morning calls.

Timing is quickly involved in marketing. Much retail promotion is based on timing. Retailers time their special sales to break with pay days in the community. Retailers make mass appeals to parents at school-opening time. Food retailers time special events for holidays, etc. Take-charge salesmen beat the sag in their sales volume by cultivating this profitable sense of timing.

Five simple rules apply in cultivating a sense of timing in take-charge selling:

1. *SYSTEMATIZE*—Good timing requires good planning. It

requires an appreciation of the value of minutes and hours. Good timing saves time. The easy-going attitude of, "I'll get at this as soon as I can," won't get it done. Good timing requires a positive, affirmative system of getting sales. This system calls for action—to get it done now, not when it's convenient.

2. *SET UP YOUR OWN TIMETABLE*—Lay down a challenge to yourself. Commit yourself to do something at a specified time. Set up your own timetable. Time your sales calls. When you make an appointment for 2 p.m. be there at 1:55. No doubt you have already developed a keen sense of timing in some things. For instance, you get to your club or to a favorite restaurant for luncheon on time. Why not be as punctual in selling? How about your other appointments for the day which could mean added sales volume for you? Good timing will get things done for you on time if you adhere to a well-planned timetable. Other take-charge salesmen are profiting by good timing every day.

3. *BUDGET YOUR TIME*—Budgeting your time is similar to budgeting your money. You plan to spend a certain number of dollars at a certain time for a certain purpose. That's money-budgeting. You plan to do certain things, to accomplish certain tasks, to attain certain objectives at a specified time. That's the art of budgeting your time. It provides a timetable for you in selling.

4. *COMBINE "WHEN" WITH "HOW"*—For major accomplishment, for progress in selling, lay your plans so you will know *HOW* you are going to attain a certain worthwhile objective. Supplement this positive method of planning with a positive deadline. A deadline becomes a fixed challenge to you to keep pushing ahead so you will arrive at your well-defined objective at a specified time. In this way you eliminate the sales hazard of uncertainty, of willy-nilly work habits.

5. *MAINTAIN "WHEN" IN TOP PRIORITY SPOT*—When you make take-charge selling a persuasive driving force it results in gains in sales volume. The record is quite clear on the persuasive power in a set time for reaching a goal. The principle of why we should maintain *"when"* in the top priority spot in take-charge selling is this: "Be in the right

place, at the right time, with the right angle, on the right product."

Women's intuition often gets the credit for good timing in domestic affairs. One take-charge saleswoman who represented an exclusive art calendar house chose the day the executive board of a much-desired account met to go after that firm's business. "I decided to convince the brains of that outfit instead of wasting time with the buyer who was indecisive and had only limited authority," she explained. That woman put fire into her presentation to the board. She combined feminine attractiveness, feminine poise and good timing to achieve maximum sales impact. She landed that worthwhile account by doing the unusual and by good timing. In response to a compliment for her achievement she said: "I got the idea from the first verse of the third chapter of Ecclesiastes in the Old Testament. There I read: "To everything there is a season, and a time to every purpose under heaven."

Good timing is so vital in selling that it appeals to take-charge salesmen. Timing is defined as the act or art of regulating the speed of performance so as to assure maximum effectiveness. Good timing holds the key to extracting the maximum profitable sales volume from the minutes and hours which are allotted to take-charge salesmen.

HOW TO MAKE CALLS MORE PRODUCTIVE

When you opened the door to your last prospect's office or home you had at your immediate disposal probably three minutes to put across the idea you had in mind that you hoped would clinch a sale. In those three minutes you may have captured your prospect's attention. You may have created interest in what you had to sell. Your prospect may have given you the green light to go ahead with your presentation. If this is the way it happened to you then those first three minutes were productive.

Those three vital minutes when you were in the presence of your prospect may have turned out to be the most profitable three minutes of your day. In those three minutes you were on trial before your prospect. You were also on trial before yourself. Now, as your own judge, you may find it profitable to honestly answer two questions:

(a) How well had you prepared to make time work for you in those first three vital minutes?

(b) How well had you prepared to make your call produce a sale?

An insurance salesman who climbed out of the slim diet of the breaking-in period to attain membership in the million-dollar club revealed the secret of his success in one word: *HUSTLE.* "Only by intelligent hustling does one gain sales," he said. "Hustling is a way of saving time and selling what I have to sell. I plan to make each call produce. I classify each prospect on my first call. If he or she doesn't qualify to buy what I have to sell I forget about him or her as an immediate prospect. If they can't qualify I'm wasting time—their time and mine—to go farther. I can't afford to waste time. When I call on a prospect whom I have previously classified I go to him or to her with a well-worked-out proposal on which I have become thoroughly sold myself. Advance planning saves time for me. It also makes my calls more productive."

The sales director of one of the West's largest movers paid tribute to his sales staff in this way:

> In our business of moving things and people from place to place we are up against stiff competition. Every salesman we have is a producer. They go after business with the self-conviction that we can serve our customers better than anyone else. Our salesmen are enthusiastic men. They make their calls productive. Their success is largely due to the fact that they enjoy their work. They have never given evidence that 40 hours a week is the limit of their productive time.

A direct salesman left his teaching position and began ringing doorbells and knocking on office doors because he believed that in the freedom of direct selling he could better achieve his personal objectives. He succeeded. His timing was right. He made the transition at an age when he had within him the fire of enthusiasm. His success formula is simple. This is the way he outlined it:

> I aim to make each call productive. My whole objective in making a call is to sell, not to visit. I have built sales volume in this way. I propose to continue to do this by persuading each prospect to buy what I have to sell in order to benefit himself. That's my primary sales pitch. That compels me to get sold on everything in my line and to offer it only insofar as I am convinced that it will fit into a prospect's needs or wants. I open

up with an attention-getter of some sort. I try to stir up anticipation, expectancy and enthusiasm in my product. Achieving this I move into a demonstration, hammering away on what my product can mean to my prospect. When I detect that I have registered conviction I get into the decision-making business of closing the sale.

Experience has taught me that there are few short cuts to closing a sale. An office supply salesman said he asked for the order at every opportunity during his presentation. He said he held himself ready to cease demonstrating any piece of office equipment he was selling if he detected that the closing moment had arrived. Case histories indicate that success in selling depends heavily on developing a sense of timing in closing to make each call productive.

HOW TO COMBAT TIME-KILLING BY YOU AND BY YOUR PROSPECTS

Day after day this problem is flung at salesmen: How to make time work for them at maximum productiveness. In solving this problem the take-charge salesman first recognizes his own time-killing habits and then attacks them. He then goes to foil the time-killing attempts of his prospects. At this point the time-conserving take-charge salesman strives to convert time-killing into sales. This is a large order, but take-charge salesmen are doing it every day. They are doing it by compressing minutes into productive units in which to make sales. For example, here we have a glimpse of the problem we face in combatting time-killers, whether the time-killers are ourselves or our prospects:

1. *THE OBJECTIVE OF THE TAKE-CHARGE SALESMAN* (a) To take command of the situation and push on until a sale results. (b) To make the minutes allotted to him yield their maximum sales potential.
2. *THE OBJECTIVE OF THE RELUCTANT PROSPECT* (a) To resist the pressure of a persuasive salesman. (b) To avoid commitment, to delay buying, to dicker, to side-step a definite decision.
3. *THE SALES HAZARDS INVOLVED IN BOTH OBJECTIVES* (a) The salesman's own inclination to "take it easy." The temptation to kill time by small talk and forgetting that he came in to sell. (b) The prospect's inclination to lead the

salesman away from his objective and the prospect's desire to kill time rather than to get down to business.

A fashion-line salesman in women's wear developed this rather simple process for combatting time-killing: "When a prospect tries to derail me I permit him to have his say and then I move in to turn the time-killing into action. This amounts to a polite way of ignoring the time-killer. If I slip and momentarily respond to any sort of time-killing by the prospect I try to quickly reverse myself. I take command of the situation to get the selling process back on the track. I have known time-killers whose main objective was to out-think and out-maneuver a salesman. My attitude is to do more than combat the time-killer. I want to sell to him. I try to change his way of thinking for one reason only: I have come there to sell and I propose to persist in trying to do just that before I take my leave."

A successful sales-training director with a background of experience in selling tangibles and also intangibles, suggests the following five methods of habitual time-killers in trying to upset salesmen:

1. By distracting the salesman.
2. By digressing during demonstration or presentation.
3. By breaking into a salesman's presentation with a racy story which he is "sure the salesman will want to hear."
4. By using the cup of coffee technique to escape from sales pressure to make a buying decision.
5. By trying to outsell the salesman.

Arthur Brisbane, one of the journalistic strong men with firm persuasive qualities, offered this thought which has motivated other ambitious take-charge salesmen: "Every moment that you save by making it useful, more profitable, is so much added to your life and its possibilities."

A sales manager in the "before need" field of mortuary and burial service comes up with four "weapons" which he says he has found to be effective in combatting time-killers. Here they are:

(a) Holding the line by a planned sales offensive.
(b) Concentrating on the sales objective.
(c) Making coffee breaks and other so-called rest periods purposeful and sales promoting in lieu of being time-killers.
(d) Resisting the temptation to let down on optimism and enthusiasm.

Benjamin Franklin, who was sales-minded and persuasive in his operations, said: "Do not squander time for that is the stuff life is made of." And, Robert M. Hutchins, the dynamic former president of Chicago University, delivered a powerful sales punch in putting across his ideas. He offered this thought in time-management: "More free time means more time to waste."

Sales records show that the habit of killing time, and the temptation for both prospects and salesmen to kill time, can be combatted by bold selling. Salesmen who take command of sales situations have demonstrated by their performance that bold selling places them in a strategic position for crushing the plague of time-killing.

HOW TO AVOID COOLING YOUR HEELS BY ADVANCE PLANNING

"Cooling your heels" is rated as one of the great time-wasters in selling. Only occasionally do long waits in a prospect's reception room pay off. Experienced take-charge salesmen have concluded that there is a better way than submitting to it.

Take-charge salesmen generally agree that a realistic schedule of calls to be made is a beginning toward cutting down the "heel-cooling" periods. These same take-charge salesmen have come up with suggestions such as these:

(a) To avoid cooling your heels learn more about your prospects' work habits. Plan to call on them during their low-pressure hours. Friendly secretaries can often be persuaded to tip you off on what is your prospect's lowest pressure time.

(b) To combat cooling your heels phone ahead (even a day ahead) for an appointment. Then, be there ahead of the scheduled time. If you should then get the heel-cooling treatment remind the prospect's secretary that you had an appointment at, say, 10 o'clock. You might say to her: "I have other appointments. It is now 10:10. Unless I can present this important matter to Mr. Smith very soon I'll have to pass it up, although I know he wants to look it over." Whether you get in to see Mr. Smith or not, you have established yourself as a busy salesman who does not waste time in purposeless waiting. In many instances this alone has selling power.

(c) To combat cooling your heels review your daily sales logs. (You should keep them up to date.) Determine from those logs what calls were productive . . . and why they were productive . . . and what calls were unproductive . . . and why they fell flat. Such reviews often throw light on sales problems. They can assist you in making your future planning more realistic and more profitable sales-wise.

(d) To combat cooling your heels group your calls. Get them close together. This saves time. It reduces the number of long jumps from prospect to prospect. By grouping calls in this way you find it easier to keep your appointments on schedule. There is sales power in becoming known as an on-time-salesman. There is a sales hazard involved in being late for an appointment.

If we understand why some prospects habitually cause salesmen to wait we can do more effective planning of our calls. A salesman who has spent a quarter of a century working in many areas and handling many lines of products has come to the following conclusion about why prospects have you cool your heels:

"Some prospects deliberately cause a salesman to wait," this salesman declared. "They get a certain amount of satisfaction in doing this. They feel that they are in the driver's seat and that you, the salesman, are bending to their will. Other prospects cause salesmen to wait because they shrink from facing up to sales pressure. Those prospects are hopeful that you, waiting to see them, will weaken, give up and get out. Other prospects simply say to a secretary or an assistant: 'Tell that salesman we don't need anything today.' This, too, is a dodge, but it leaves the door wide open for a take-charge salesman to drive in with a persuasive appeal to his wants, not his needs. Still other prospects are frank enough to pass the word to the salesman that they are tied up and can't see them at that time. This cuts the salesman loose, leaving the door wide open for a return call at a time convenient to both."

HOW TO DEVELOP THE ART OF SELF-MOTIVATION

"All problems confronting us should be considered improvement opportunities," said Golden K. Driggs, business executive. In this, Mr. Driggs, consciously or otherwise, turned the spotlight on those among us who sell to keep the wheels of industry turning. In Mr.

Driggs' statement the importance of self-motivation is brought into sharp focus for take-charge salesmen.

John Drinkwater poetically wrote: "Grant us the purpose, ribbed and edged with steel, to strike the blow." In this, too, take-charge salesmen in every field may find inspiration for developing the art of self-motivation.

A highly productive sales executive stole the show in a sales seminar attended by sales people representing a wide range of products and services. That young executive, billed as one of several speakers on the program, took command of the situation and poured out a two-fisted challenge which is still ringing in the ears of many of his listeners. He said:

> All of you have heard about what they call self-motivation. Most of you have brushed the term out of your minds much as you would get rid of a pesky fly. But, self-motivation is what you get out of a first-class job of goal-setting, followed up by a first-class job of selling. Self-motivation means that you are giving yourself a kick in the pants to get you off your dime and swing into the big time in selling. The best shot in the arm that you can get is to set up a tempting goal for yourself. Make that goal so attractive that you will stretch out eagerly to reach it. Make that goal enticing enough that you will promise yourself in all seriousness that you will hit that high figure in sales production which you have set up to pull you upward by your bootstraps. Get fired up about your goal. Go after the prospects you have been neglecting. Go after new accounts you may have ignored. Over and over again remind yourself of the promise you have made to yourself that you will go out against hell and high water to pile up more sales volume than you did yesterday. Then believe firmly that you can do it. This is not baloney. This is the tonic you and I require to knock us off dead center, to motivate us to plunge into the market place and demonstrate that we really do rate high as sales people.

Development of the art of self-motivation requires that we:

(a) Set up a target for ourselves with enticing figures on it.
(b) Get all fired up about the greatness of the opportunity we have created for ourselves by setting up an enticing and attainable objective.
(c) Commit ourselves to combat time-killers and time-killing habits and make every minute of the day more productive.

When we have accomplished the foregoing A, B, C's, our next step toward the fullness of self-motivation is to pour additional fuel on our self-ignited fire of enthusiasm for selling.

HOW TO DEVELOP SELF-INCENTIVES WITH TAKE-CHARGE SELLING IMPACT

A salesman of the rugged "go-get-'em" type was asked by several of his associates how he managed to build up his prospect list and how he succeeded in selling so many of those prospects. He replied:

> I need constant encouragement. The only way I have found to get that encouragement is to develop it within myself. I search for an incentive. I find that the incentive I develop for myself is the most workable and the most productive. For instance, nothing stimulates me quite as well as my first sale of the day. So, to begin my day I turn my full persuasive power on the prospect I have specially selected for my first call. By selling to him I get wound up for a productive day. In this way I develop my own incentives. This method has been profitable for me. I sell advertising. I turn in a respectable volume regularly. I am not a 'milk toast' salesman. I go in to sell. To my prospects I point to the record which shows that the investment made by big, consistent advertisers pays off in great sales volume. I make my prospects hungry for more business. When I convince them that my idea is sound they buy. Each prospect on my list becomes an individual incentive for me to sell to him.

One firm puts this enticing appeal out for prospective salesmen: "A very large segment of top management is recruited from the personnel having the ability, the techniques and the know-how to handle sales problems. This may be your opportunity to enter this rapidly expanding industry." Such an inducement provides an incentive for sales people to better themselves. In turn, the self-incentives of those sales people may arouse them to get out and prove to themselves that they have the capacity for greater production in sales.

Among the self-incentives which have take-charge selling impact are these:

1. *HOPE*—The great salesmen of record have been and are hopeful men. They are optimists. They rebel against negative thinking. Martin Luther said: "Everything that is done in

the world is done by hope." As salesmen we wake up each morning with the hope that it will be a better day than yesterday, that it will prove to be fruitful for us.

2. *WANT*—At a sales conference one day a jewelry salesman made this point: "A salesman on the road has wants just as his prospects and customers have wants. A salesman's wants stimulate him to satisfy those wants. The wants of his prospects stimulate the salesman to supply those wants. The wants of salesmen, their prospects, and their customers provide the incentives which stimulate salesmen to become top producers. Wants are the substance from which take-charge salesmen develop many of their self-incentives with sales impact.

3. *DESIRE*—After want becomes strong enough desire takes over. By developing strong self-incentives they goad us to act. At that point take-charge selling unwinds in full force. First want, then desire, then an incentive has come into being. As Vince Lombardi, the football coach, said: "Winning isn't everything, but wanting to win is." So it is with selling. Wanting to sell is the dynamic force which develops strong self-incentives with take-charge selling impact.

Consider and apply the following tested ways in which self-incentives have been developed with take-charge selling impact:

(a) By capitalizing on the desire to enjoy a brighter and more prosperous future.

(b) By capitalizing on a desire to serve customers so well that they will repeat and repeat and will suggest prospects who may be developed into active customers and thereby, we hope, adding a new account daily to profit the salesman.

(c) By turning to big thinking, as a small-order salesman did and thereby topped his previous selling average by landing a $2,500 order. That victory for that salesman developed within him a self-incentive for greater achievement in selling.

(d) By emulating the spirit of a veteran calendar salesman who wrote his forty-fifth consecutive annual calendar order for a bank.

(e) By recognizing that bold selling in itself generates self-incentives; that it is the means by which take-charge sales-

men satisfy and profit by their own and their prospects'
hopes, their wants and their desires. Those take-charge
salesmen capitalize on the time which is allotted to them
each day by making that time work for them at top sales
production speed.

A real estate salesman for years maintained just an average record.
"A living," he called it. Then he struck an upward stride. He became
a consistent high-producing salesman. "All I needed," he explained,
"was an incentive, and the incentives I created for myself proved to
be the best. They had greater sales impact because I believed in
them."

HOW TO CREATE A GOOD SELLING CLIMATE BY
DEVELOPING AN ATTITUDE OF SUCCESS

Favorable timing and the development of a favorable selling climate set the stage for effective sales presentations. The sales manager
of an investment firm paid tribute to one of his consistently high
producers in this way:

"Jim has that special touch in his personality which enables him
to create a warm selling climate. He gets the chill out of the air. Too
often we find that a chill does come over a selling situation and
develops into a killing frost. Not so with Jim. He has the gift of
drawing people to him. He radiates success and good will."

What this amounts to, according to that sales manager, is better
communication. He related an experiment he had made with favorable results. He passed on to Jim the names of several prospects who
had been classified as "impossible" by other salesmen. A high per-
centage of those "impossible" prospects yielded to Jim's persuasiveness and bought.

Here are five ways in which you can create a good selling climate.
You probably can think of additional ways. But, consider the following factors which have been tried and have created a good selling
climate for other take-charge salesmen:

1. Capture your prospect's interest. Develop personal magnet-
   ism. Show interest in your prospect, his business and his
   welfare.
2. Develop a sense of timing. Favorably impress your prospect.
   Show consideration for his time. Conserve your own time.
   Make time work for you.

3. Exploit the possibilities for benefits for your prospect in what you have to sell. Use take-charge showmanship for more dynamic sales presentations.
4. Be enthusiastic. Show sincere personal interest in your prospect's plans and objectives.
5. Take command of each sales situation. Demonstrate that you are warmly sincere. Get close to your prospect. Win his confidence. Be on the level with him. Become so friendly and convincing that your prospect will believe that you are on his team.

A specialty salesman became known as a friend-maker for himself and for the house he represented. He made the following significant point about handling hard-to-handle customers and how to create a good selling climate:

"Arguing with a customer is a useless and expensive luxury," he said. "If I win the argument I probably will lose the sale and also a friend. There may be satisfaction in telling off an ornery prospect or customer. Nevertheless, the price is high. I suggest another way: Tame him. Step into his shoes and see things from his side of the street. I may pat an ornery prospect on the back, speak calmly to him, speak kindly and persuasively. I get downright pleasant in some situations. Many times the most ornery prospect responds to persuasion and winds up eating out of my hand. Then I have won, not an argument, but a sale, and a friend, all by improving communication. That's what I call creating a good selling climate."

The principle: Courtesy, gentleness, calmness and sincerity never downgrade a salesman. Customers love it. So do prospects. In this way a warm, favorable climate is created in which sales can take root and thrive.

CHAPTER NINE

HOW TO CONVERT CALL-BACKS INTO SALES VOLUME

The furnishings of your living room probably include an electronic device which has a three-fold purpose: (a) To inform; (b) to entertain; (c) *TO SELL.* Your TV screen shows and the accompanying voice tells. By this dual impact a desire is created within you to buy or to invest. Your radio, too, tells but it does not show. It has ear appeal but no eye appeal, both of which have impact in selling.

The sales power of TV and radio is, in large measure, due to repetition. Over and over again commercial spots drum away on selected themes. That is effective salesmanship. Persistent repetition has demonstrated itself to be effective. The evidence contained in case records is convincing that sales do result from telling and retelling the advertiser's story when it is done appealingly and persuasively. This, then, becomes a dynamic force in generating desire for a product or service.

The same sales power is present in print advertising. In newspapers and magazines the sales message can be read. Accompanying the message with illustration shows *HOW* the product or service can become beneficial to the prospective buyer, who, incidentally, is

139

reading the message. But the significant thing from the standpoint of effective salesmanship is that print advertising is also repeated because experience has taught us that repetition has selling power.

Call-backs fall into the pattern of repetition for effect. By calling back on a prospect the take-charge salesman stimulates desire for something he has to sell. For instance, we may call on Mr. Prospect today and get only fleeting attention from him. So it is when we flip on our TV's and the first commercial fails to stir us out of our relaxed comfort in our easy chairs. But, when we call again on Mr. Prospect and retell our sales story we often may stir up interest. We may tell our story a little better, a little more realistically, a little more colorfully than we did on the first call. We may aim our sales pitch more directly at the heart of our prospect—at his self-interest. Thus we may succeed in getting a little more consideration from Mr. Prospect.

Perhaps it may require two, or three, or four call-backs to arouse Mr. Prospect to the full desirability of possessing our product or taking on our service. However, as take-charge salesmen we persist in making those call-backs. We do this for the same reason that TV commercials tell us and show us, and retell and reshow.

Take-charge selling is not a one shot deal. Those in the big figure class, those who think big and sell boldly, convert call-backs into sales volume. They refuse to accept "no" as a prospect's final decision. They go back to him again and again, determined to change his mind.

The principle: Call-backs generate greater sales power by purposeful repetition.

Take-charge salesmen use well-planned call-backs as a vital part of their over-all selling program. They chart their call-backs as they do their first calls. They do advance planning on call-backs to make them more effective, more productive. Take-charge salesmen rarely write off a desirable prospect as "impossible" merely because they have failed to get an order on the first few calls. They become steamed up themselves, determined to find the approach that will swing the reluctant prospect over to their side. They rely heavily on purposeful repetition, on well-planned call-backs, on bold selling to sell to that challenging prospect.

HOW TO GENERATE TAKE-COMMAND SALES POWER IN CALL-BACKS

A factory-trained expediter, employed by one of America's popular medium-priced car makers, switched to sales and in a few years established a record in new customer business. He attributed his success to call-backs. He said: "It's useless to call back on a prospect unless you have a good reason for taking up his time. In a call-back you have to have something important for your prospect to shoot at. Preparation for a call-back is much more important than for a first call."

This expediter-turned-salesman, who found a way to get business where others considered the sales possibilities to be lost, set down the following reasons for making return calls on prospective automobile buyers:

(a) To sell a new car to a new account.

(b) To project a new idea with sales impact.

(c) To get closer to the prospect than he succeeded in doing on previous calls.

(d) To strengthen the prospect's confidence in the car he was selling and also to win the prospect's confidence in himself as a salesman.

(e) To find out more about how his prospect thinks, how he works, what his ideas are about cars and about methods of doing business.

(f) To produce persuasive evidence that he has a great automobile value.

(g) To get the names of those with whom his prospect associates and find out what their preferences are for cars.

(h) To stir up enthusiasm in his prospect for a new car, especially for the car which he is selling.

Call-backs amount to reserve selling power for take-charge salesmen. Those who devise an orderly system of making call-backs never run short of prospects. "The prospect who turned me down today becomes a challenge for me to sell to him tomorrow," said an outdoor advertising salesman. "I go back to the man who has previously turned me down with a new approach, based on a new idea, or a modification of an old idea, or with strong evidence of how someone in the same line of business as my prospect has cashed in by judiciously using billboard advertising. When I discovered that my call-backs required more persuasive selling than my first calls I began to close sales. I learned that the secret of success in call-backs lies in building up a prospect's enthusiasm for what I have to sell."

Take-charge salesmen who have captured sales which were once thought to be lost have become successful by: (a) literally picking up the wreckage of lost sales; (b) returning to their prospects under a fresh head of steam and converting those prospects to the idea that buying was to their advantage.

In the battle for business we who fight to sell can detect something of sales significance in the philosophy of James J. Corbett, the great heavyweight boxer. Said Corbett: "When your feet are so tired that you have to shuffle back to the center of the ring, fight one more round." This may be the secret of sales success in purposeful call-backs. It is typical of the spirit of take-charge salesmen who build up sales volume by getting back into the center of the ring for one more round.

HOW TO CASH IN WITH AN APPEALING, VITAL OBJECTIVE IN YOUR CALL-BACKS

In the conference room of an advertising agency the following suggestion was prominently displayed: "Any salesman worthy of the name should be able to present an idea with self-interest appeal to the average business man on every call."

An insurance salesman said call-backs provide him with greater opportunities than first calls. "The ice is broken on the first call," he said. "On the call-back I concentrate on an appeal that will swing my prospect around to thinking about the part insurance can play in his life."

The call-back you are about to make deserves the same, or better advance planning than you gave to your initial call on that prospect. Or was it because you did not fully prepare for that call that your prospect's flame of interest flickered and died out? Your call-back can, with proper preparation, eliminate most of the sales hazards which may have prevented you from closing sales on the first call. As take-charge salesmen of experience we can testify that you can neutralize sales hazards which, in fact, were responsible for creating new opportunities to close sales on call-backs. A sales hazard, perhaps a temporary one, may have challenged you to go back to that prospect. For this reason this repeat call seemed to whisper to you: "Prepare yourself to overcome all sales hazards on this call-back. Go in boldly to sell!"

The following elements are involved if we would make our call-backs produce sales:

1. *SET UP AN OBJECTIVE*—Have a valid reason for making the call-back. Have a workable plan.
2. *PRESENT AN IDEA*—A well-defined idea has sales punch. Make it specific. Nothing vague.
3. *DRAMATIZE THE IDEA*—Dress it up. Make it attractive. Make it tempting. Make it persuasive. Make it convincing to the prospect.

The foregoing is not as complex as it might appear to be. Take the food industry, for example. You may be selling display cases or roll-in carts for conveying eggs, or other products. As a take-charge salesman selling such equipment to food dealers you would take into account such things as time to be saved. You would present experience data to your time-conscious prospect and you would show him how other time-conscious dealers have, for instance, rolled 117 dozen eggs into display space in about 41 seconds. You now have his interest. You have touched a sensitive nerve—the financial nerve which responds to time, speed, convenience, more sales, more profits, etc. That prospect wants to know all about the money-making possibilities of the equipment you have for sale. It may require a call-back or two to break down all of that prospect's sales resistance, but if you eventually succeed in closing the sale those call-backs will have been worth your effort.

An appealing vital objective becomes the heart of any effective call-back. The insurance salesman called again on his prospect to convince him that it would be to his advantage to become more adequately insured. The automobile salesman called back with a two-pronged objective: (a) To convince his prospect of the advantage to him of buying a new car; and (b) to convince that prospect that the car the salesman was selling was the most desirable on the market for his purpose and within his price range.

To simplify the successful call-back formula we need to ask ourselves three questions and answer them fully and in detail prior to making the return call upon our prospect:

(a) *WHY* am I again calling on this prospect?
(b) *WHAT* will be my most persuasive approach? What will stimulate my prospect to become excited over my idea or my product?
(c) *HOW* can I best persuade my prospect to act, *TO BUY?*

HOW TO PROFIT BY CREATING A FAVORABLE IMAGE ON YOUR CALL-BACKS

A few real image-makers made the circuit in the not too distant past. They set up shop in community streets and hawked their wares. They sold cure-all nostrums and glittering "diamonds" at "half price." These peddlers created an image, but it was the wrong image for creating prestige for professional salesmen. In time the adverse image faded. It lost out as a constructive sales promoting force. Today's objective in take-charge selling is to create a favorable image. We strive to do this on first calls and also on call-backs. In doing this we build prestige by developing such qualities as these:

- (a) *PERSONAL APPEARANCE*—We dress conservatively and well. We have a clean, neat appearance.
- (b) *MANNERISM*—We conduct ourselves in such a way that attention is centered on our prospects and not on ourselves. We avoid being show-offs. We recognize that show-offs did well as side-show barkers but they seldom do well in today's busy, discriminating and competitive market.
- (c) *SPEECH*—We practice self-control. We modulate our voices. We try to become persuasive by speaking clearly and being precise.
- (d) *PERSONALITY*—To become more persuasive we are pleasant, considerate. We remain friendly even in the clinches.
- (e) *KNOWLEDGEABLE*—We read and observe to become well-informed. We reach out to our prospects. We go in armed with abundant facts to convince the prospect that what we have to sell can benefit him in some way and induce him to buy.

Fred Gilbert was a successful specialty salesman. He created an image of success. His clothes were tailored. He was clean-shaven, his shoes were polished, his shirt was clean. He wore attractive ties. When Fred came in the prospect usually was favorably impressed. Fred's approach was natural, never affected. He disliked prima donnas in selling. He spoke up, sweetening his words with a smile. He created the impression that he knew his business. He was an idea man, pleasant, considerate and helpful. Eventually he was plucked out of the many salesmen in his firm to become a district salesmanager. He succeeded there, too. He taught his sales staff how they could profit by creating favorable images on calls and also on call-backs.

One of Fred's salesmen who had upped his sales volume explained his gain in this way:

> I took it seriously when the chief put it to us so straight that call-backs were never routine. With that some of us got wise to how we had been missing the boat on call-backs. Somehow we had been operating with the mistaken idea that call-backs were something the head office expected of us and that it was our duty to drop in on those prospects we hadn't been able to land just to check the visit off on our reports. We had done our good turn for the day. In time I saw that my call-backs were not paying off. So I tried Fred Gilbert's system. I tried to sell harder on a call-back than I had on the first call. In time it got through to me that if I didn't get business on a first call, or a second call, that it was probably because I hadn't been persuasive enough. So I changed my whole idea about call-backs and then they began to pay off for me. I suppose I improved my image. I hope so. It seems to me that the test of an improved image in selling is whether you succeed in closing sales on call-backs. I have found that call-backs can result in reestablishing friendly and productive relationships with prospects who had been on my non-productive list.

HOW TAKE-CHARGE SALESMEN BUILD SALES VOLUME BY THE "GRIN AND BEAR IT" TECHNIQUE

The simplicity of the "grin and bear it" technique in take-charge selling is made clear by a man who explained to his colleagues how he built sales volume by this method. He said: "My record of sales proves to my own satisfaction that doors that have been closed, even those that have been slammed shut, can be reopened and sales made by aggressive, knowledgeable salesmanship."

The "grin and bear it" attitude in selling is closely allied to the principle of pumping life into dying prospects by making call-backs intelligently.

A training director told his group of candidates for sales careers that they should be prepared to "meet rebuff after rebuff with broader and broader grins." He hammered away on the doctrine of bold selling. He tried to open the eyes of men who yearned for success in selling. His objective: To enable them to detect un-developed opportunities, even in those repeated rebuffs. He admonished his student-salesmen to "grin and bear it."

This training director maintained that the "grin and bear it" technique is sound. He assured his class that this attitude is indicative of persistent determination and has developed sales volume for others, and it can do as much for them. He disclosed his own sales record which supported his claim that the "grin and bear it" method of selling is based on: (a) courage; (b) resolution; (c) self-discipline.

One of the student salesmen asked: "Why shouldn't I blow up when an ornery prospect insults me and my product?"

The sales training director replied: "It all depends upon what your ultimate objective in selling is. What goals you have set." He then added: "Will Rogers had the best answer to your question that I've heard. He said: 'People who fly into a rage always make a bad landing.' My point is this: Your ornery prospect would have been totally disarmed if you had remained calm, permitted him to explode, and then if you had very pleasantly moved into a strong sales pitch. The principle remains the same: Grin and bear it. This principle produces sales and, after all, this is the primary purpose of salesmanship."

A veteran salesman contended that what is called a "seller's market" seldom develops top level salesmen. "Easy going softens us," he said. "We get to expecting too much for too little. The best thing that ever happened to me in selling was when a prospect slammed the door on me and told me to get out. This left me with two alternatives: (1) write that man off as a deadbeat prospect, or (2) figure out a way to penetrate his shell and sell to him. I chose the latter course, to grin and bear it. Result: My return call was a pleasant experience. No reference was made by either of us to the previous unpleasant call. I presented an attractive idea to him and he went for it. He has been buying from me ever since and today we are close friends. In addition my total sales volume is greater than before I decided to grin and bear it."

Passion is something to be controlled in selling, according to another high-producing take-charge salesman in the drug industry. He maintains that "if you can't grin and bear it you better look for smoother sailing elsewhere, because salesmanship is a robust calling."

William Penn had a slant on passion which might be relevant in considering the "grin and bear it" technique in selling. Penn said: "Passion is a sort of fever. It deprives us of the use of our judgment; for it raises a dust very hard to see through."

THREE SALES-PRODUCING WAYS FOR FOLLOWING THROUGH ON CALL-BACKS

In virtually every line call-backs have proved to be the backbone of sales building systems. Call-backs yield higher incomes and greater prestige for take-charge salesmen.

A well-known salesman in the duplicating machine field rates call-backs as his most productive calls. "When I dropped the notion that call-backs were routine things that had to be done, I began to make them pay off," he said. "To follow through on every call is the secret of making call-backs pay," he added. "Too often some of us close a sale and take that customer off our active list. I have learned to keep that sort of customer on my active prospect list and to develop him by following through with call-backs. You see, he has been introduced to my product. My groundwork has been laid with him. It now becomes vital for me to find out if all is well with the equipment I sold to him. Is it measuring up to his expectations? A follow-through call can clear the air if something has gone haywire. If all is well my customer is wide open for buying more of my products. I suggest that salesmen should never underrate the selling power of following through on sales they have made."

What then are the best methods of maintaining contact with prospects and with established accounts? Three standard methods have top priority because they have been tested. They have been the means by which salesmen have built up sales volume. Here they are:

1. *WELL-TIMED CALL-BACKS.*
2. *WELL-TIMED PHONE CALLS.*
3. *WELL-TIMED LETTERS.*

The follow-through is closely related to the call-back. In both instances the objective is to develop business. This simplifies the purpose. When salesmen follow through with a vigorous take-charge spirit they usually sell. Case records support this claim. The call-back is one form of following through. In call-backs we strive to pump life into a dying sale. In the follow-through we are indicating to a customer that we are sincerely interested in him and in his business.

We are letting him know that nis satisfaction or dissatisfaction is important to us. We want to convince him that he is the most important customer on our list and treat him as if he were. This is take-charge salesmanship in action to build sales volume.

Salesman "A," for instance, opened up a new territory for a food products house he represented. He considered this to be an opportunity and a challenge. The leading competitor of Salesman "A's" firm had virtually given up the territory. Salesman "A" had an idea that gourmet food with prestige appeal could be popularized in that area and he proposed to do just that. He chose three accounts on which to concentrate his sales fire. He persuaded one of those prospects to take on his line. He also induced him to set up a gourmet section in the traffic area of his market. He volunteered to be on hand for the opening of this section and to assist the store manager in making it a promotional event. This got the customer excited. The result: Sales were good. People talked about the exotic foods featured in that market. Salesman "A" kept in touch with the situation by mail, by frequent phone calls and in a few weeks he followed through with a personal call. By that time the word had spread about the gourmet section in that one market. Salesman "A's" other prospective accounts in non-competitive sections of his territory were ready to take on his line.

By following through on his accounts Salesman "A" succeeded in developing his territory into a high-profit producer for him and for the firm he represented. And, incidentally, for those to whom he had sold his product and his ideas.

Take-charge salesmen who have mastered the art of following through and making call-backs with a well-defined purpose become most persuasive in their selling. They profit by keeping in touch with prospects, with established accounts and with market developments in the territory they cover. They check on what has been ordered to find out if it came through in good shape. They check on resale merchandise to find out how it has been moving out of their customers' stores. They check on how strong their customers are pushing the products the salesmen have sold to them. They try to make sure that those they serve are happy and that they feel that they have been benefited. By keeping in close touch they are in position to detect brewing trouble and dissatisfaction and to take remedial action in time to save the situation.

HOW TO STEAM UP YOUR TAKE-CHARGE SELLING POWER WITH THE TRIPLE STRENGTH IN ADVERTISING, IMAGE-MAKING AND FRESH IDEAS

A steady climber in sales production whom I knew as Jack Carter discovered that he could capitalize greatly by using product advertising as a support factor in selling. When one of the top lines of ball point pens broke into print with color advertising and persuasive copy to promote their product, Jack saw great sales possibilities in this campaign. This is how he seized the opportunity to capitalize on those factory ads:

> I picked up several magazines carrying those ball point ads and began making calls on prospects whom I had been nudging to buy ball points in quantity. When I laid a magazine on a prospect's desk I noticed that I had his attention. Then I directed his attention to the selling points brought out in the advertisement. Doing this, I detected that I had accomplished three things:
>
> 1. I had captured the favorable attention of my prospect. He began to read the message. Then he got interested in the in-use illustration in the ad. This provided me with a good base for launching my sales pitch.
> 2. I had created a favorable impression of myself and my product. My prospect was pleased by my interest in how he might profit by expanding the sale of ball points. He agreed that he could probably widen his market and he turned back again to reread the advertisement.
> 3. The ad opened up communication lines between me and my prospects. Fresh ideas popped into our minds, stimulated by the ads, and we talked about how to sell more ball points.

A wholesale tire salesman with a dynamic approach to truck fleet operators carried a special portfolio with him at all times. He kept this package up to date with current factory promotion for his line of tires. He had magazine ads in color, newspaper ads in color and in black and white, and he carried with him a schedule of all radio and television commercial spots on his line of tires to be aired in his territory. He used these aids to selling in numerous ways. He profited by using "splash" ads as door openers when going after new accounts. He used the whole advertising schedule as evidence of how his firm backed up regional dealers and how his firm put across to the buying public the quality points which created demand for his tires. In this way he created a faverable image with tire merchants and with fleet owners for his product. He impressed those potential buyers that he was a man who knew his business, and one who was interested in their welfare as well. His selling approach was simple: He came in armed with fresh ideas about: (a) how to profitably merchandise tires; (b) how to economize on tires and increase safety at the same time by using his tires, thus creating self-interest desire in the minds of his prospects.

By the self-interest approach the tire salesman also enhanced his own image with them. The ultimate result reflected in the steady climb of his sales volume.

A newspaper space advertising salesman built a notable record by steaming up his selling power by using his own product plus ideas and call-backs. For convincing, sales-promoting presentations he drew on specific advertising campaigns that had been notably successful. In these presentations, often made at board meetings, this advertising salesman became an image-maker and he made it pay off well for him. In discussing his method he made this point:

> On first calls I seldom come out with a signed contract. The worthwhile guys usually want time to think. Such thinkers are not the indecisive fellows. The thinkers I refer to are big thinkers. To impress those fellows I have to come up with fresh ideas. I have found that the constant hammering on a good idea produces sales. The call-back is a big thing in selling advertising. I try to make each call-back purposeful. I show prospects how others make their advertising pay off. I tease the appetite of a prospect until he gets downright hungry for more profitable business. When he becomes hungry enough and I have convinced him that advertising will appease his appetite then he buys, usually with enthusiastic anticipation.

CHAPTER TEN

HOW TO TAKE CHARGE WITH THE DUAL BENEFIT TECHNIQUE

What is the dual benefit technique?

It is a method or system which involves profits or other benefits for both the buyer and the seller.

This technique has lifted take-charge salesmen up above the crowd in production. By benefitting their prospects they have placed themselves in a command position and have enjoyed similar benefits themselves.

Let us take a look at a projected line-up for a sales contest in which dual benefits are possible:

1. *YOU . . . THE NO. 1 CONTENDER*—You are a take-charge salesman. The potential benefits for you are locked up in a projected sale which is challenging you. Self-interest motivates you to go after the big stake in the contest. This spirit propels you out of the ranks of run-of-the-mill sales people and into the team of take-charge salesmen who score high.

2. *YOUR PROSPECT . . . THE NO. 2 CONTENDER*—He,

too, is motivated by self-interest. He holds the keys to the benefits you are after. He resists buying. He reasons that by not buying, or by delaying his decision, he may benefit. He will abdicate his fortress of resistance only when he can be motivated by self-interest to do so. This, then, becomes your challenge: To make your sales presentation so strong, so persuasive, so convincing that your prospect will let go of his money to possess what you have to sell.

Simple as this is in principle the dual benefit technique is a personal test in most sales situations. It requires bold selling. It requires confident selling, motivated by self-interest on the part of the salesman. This suggests that we sharpen our skills in the following areas:

(a) *TO KNOW MORE ABOUT OUR PROSPECTS*—We will find out more about the needs, wants and desires of our prospects. This will give us insight into how our product or service can benefit those whom we hope to benefit by selling to them.

(b) *TO TOTALLY COVER OUR TERRITORIES*—Our own self-interest suggests that slip-shod sales methods can leave rich veins of ore exposed which competing salesmen can explore or exploit.

(c) *TO DEVELOP THE ART OF CHANGING PACE*—Our self-interest prompts us to alternate low pressure and high pressure selling to meet the challenges of shifting sales problems. We can learn to detect when to ease up and when to increase sales pressure. We learn by experience that sales pressure is a dual benefit process of assisting prospects to make decisions.

(d) *TO AVOID SALES RUTS*—Self-interest spurs us to be alert to the full potential of what we have to sell and of the market area that we are working. We have seen luke-warm salesmen sent back to the bench in sales contests because take-charge selling means bold selling. The prospect of dual benefits provides motivation to get take-charge salesmen into productive action.

(e) *TO PUT STEAM BEHIND CALL-BACKS*—Again self-interest reminds us that the prospects we failed to sell yesterday missed out on certain potential benefits. Those benefits had been within their reach had they purchased what we had to sell. Self-interest further points out to us that somehow we lacked enough steam on the previous call to close the possible sales. By being fully steamed up on call-backs we are in better position to benefit our prospects and also ourselves. The ultimate goal of the dual benefit technique is to sell.

The sales director of one of the large securities brokers had a yardstick by which he measured sales people: (a) Their record had to qualify them as producers who continued to grow in effectiveness. (b) They had to be men who welcomed demanding challenges. (c) They had to be ambitious, resourceful, imaginative, self-starting, and they had to have drive and integrity.

To take charge of a sales situation with the dual benefit technique we need to look at ourselves. To achieve sales mastery we must take charge of each sales situation. For an honest, searching self-examination let us ask ourselves these questions:

1. Am I in good health? Do I attack each sales problem with full vigor? Or is it about time that my doctor be brought into the picture? Is it possible that I might need a shot in the arm?
2. Do I make new friends every day? Do I lose a few? Why?
3. Is my voice-tone pleasant or do I irritate people in the way I make presentations? Do I have enough determination to correct my speech deficiencies with professional guidance?
4. Is my appearance impressive? Is my conduct such that people seek my company? Are the right answers to the two foregoing questions important to me?
5. Am I mentally alert to every situation that confronts me? Why not?
6. Do I radiate enthusiasm or am I easily let down? Can I deny that enthusiasm has hard-hitting sales power?

FIVE REQUIREMENTS FOR SUCCESS IN TAKE-CHARGE SELLING

As motivation for your personal development consider this quintet of sales-building qualities with which top-rated take-charge salesmen are endowed:

1. *PERSONAL DRIVE*
2. *PERSONAL INTEGRITY*
3. *SELF-STARTING ENERGY*

4. *SALES-SHARP RESOURCEFULNESS*
5. *SALES-ORIENTED IMAGINATION*

A young salesman, lacking in experience, joined a well-organized sales force and at the end of the second week came up with a score that astounded his colleagues. Most of them called it "beginner's luck." The sales manager had another idea: "I believe what you call his luck is based on personal drive. He takes the initiative and defies opposition. You'll notice that all of his business is new business. Usually new business is the fruit of personal drive."

Another salesman with several years of experience in the automotive field turned to mobile homes. He had a lead on other newcomers to the mobile home field. He had a list of prospects he had brought with him from the automobile field. He knew those people well. He talked to them about changing their way of living. They listened to this salesman because he had built a reputation with them of being a salesman of integrity. They believed in him. They told others that he had gone into selling mobile homes. His salesmanager overheard a prospect remark: "When I heard that a square guy like that automobile salesman had taken to selling these homes on wheels I decided I ought to think about buying one of them."

Case records of sales successes provide conclusive proof that personal drive plus personal integrity is a hard combination to defeat. This combination has laid firm foundations for success for many take-charge salesmen.

The drive, the integrity and the self-starting energy of salesmen on the way up in virtually every major line on the market attest to the fact that self-starting energy is a required asset for top production in selling. Self-starting energy is a quality of leadership. It enables the salesman to jump into a sales situation at the right moment and take command, passing up the slow starters in the race for sales volume.

An insurance salesman, handicapped by the loss of a leg in an accident, pulled himself up into the elite million-dollar club. As we look at his record we find that by his resourcefulness he capitalized on his personal drive, his self-starting energy and his unimpeachable integrity. He cultivated his sense of timing, his understanding of people and he took maximum advantage of sales possibilities by legitimate and creative salesmanship.

What we call "creativity" is, in fact, imagination. In selling it is the difference between developing a situation with persuasive sales appeal and slumping into routine order-writing merely to supply the "wants" of prospects. The imaginative salesman sells ideas rather than things. He sells beauty and comfort rather than a suit of clothes. He develops volume in insurance by selling peace of mind, by selling prospects on protection against disaster, by presenting sound investment possibilities. The imaginative real estate salesman dealing in homes makes his pitch on prestige living and on living comfort rather than on bricks and concrete. The imaginative salesman reaches out to touch the life of a prospect with a sales appeal that assists the prospect in making a favorable decision.

Backing up the qualities of personal drive, self-starting energy, resourcefulness and imagination is that matter of personal integrity which has a form of sales impact exclusively its own. James A. Garfield, the twentieth president of the United States, said: "I would rather be beaten in the right than succeed in the wrong." And, Ernest L. Wilkinson, distinguished educator, observed: "Whether you succeed or not will depend more upon your integrity than on your brilliance."

Walter Lippmann, distinguished journalist, might well have written the following for those of us who are engaged in selling: "You don't have to preach honesty to men with a creative purpose." Take-charge salesmanship is a creative art. It calls up the virtues of integrity, initiative, energy, resourcefulness and imagination to move products from the production line into the hands of consumers. Take-charge salesmen sell by communicating ideas to those who can benefit by those ideas.

The primary value to take-charge salesmen of the five requirements set forth as requirements for their success is that those five requirements have dynamic power for developing and sustaining sales volume.

HOW TO MAKE THE TURN-DOWN A "GO" SIGNAL

Hard selling is said to begin when the prospect shakes his head and emphatically says, "No!"

A physician I knew had a full measure of ability in take-charge selling. He had the ability to convince the most wary patient that major surgery would be a great idea. This physician did what the take-charge salesmen do. He got close to his "prospects." He won their confidence, which top-rated salesmen do. He understood the patient's reasons for hesitating about "buying" the operation idea, much as the take-charge salesman understands why his prospect is reluctant to buy his service or his product. That physician appealed to the emotions of his patients as well as to their reason. Similarly many sales are closed by laying aside logic and appealing to the emotions of a prospect.

An insurance salesman who has written contracts for me told me how he made turn-downs his "go" signals. In one instance a prospect flatly said, "No." He had been working on that prospect for some time. The salesman admitted to me that he was disappointed. He wanted that sale. He had worked hard for it. But, as he sized up the situation he decided he now had nothing to lose by boldly taking command of the situation. He made another effort to revive the prospect's interest but the prospect shut off discussion by giving the salesman another flat turn-down. With this the salesman collected his sales props and reached out his hand in a friendly gesture to the prospect. "Sorry," he said, "but I have just one question before I leave." The prospect showed new interest. "Of course," he said, "What's your question?" The salesman shot back: "What will your family do if something happens to you tonight?" The prospect had no ready answer. Finally he spoke: "It was something sudden-like that pauperized the wife of our vice-president when he was killed." The salesman hadn't known about that tragedy. However, by a simple, direct and pertinent question he reversed a sales situation. A turn-down had become his "go" signal. Instead of going out empty-handed he wrote a larger contract for the prospect than he had originally anticipated.

Follow-ups on turn-downs have a way of promoting sales. A veteran automobile salesman boasted to me that he had never had what he considered to be a final turn-down. One method this salesman uses is to remind a prospect, who has turned him down, of their meeting. At the end of the working day this enterprising veteran salesman writes personal notes on postcards on which the salesman's picture is printed. Typical of his messages to prospects who have turned him down is this note he wrote to me: "Nice of you to stop in. I'd like to serve you whenever you are ready. New cars are coming in daily now. A full selection will be on our floor this week. Drop in and look 'em over. No obligation. Bring your wife along. She'll enjoy the greatest showing of motorized comfort we have ever put on. You'll appreciate the great values we are offering right now."

Is it worth a post card and a few minutes of time to follow up in this way on a turn-down? It has been worth it for that veteran in the business who has built consistent sales volume gains by take-charge salesmanship. He meets the five requirements for success in take-charge selling. He makes turn-downs "go" signals.

Case records show that take-charge salesmen in virtually every competitive line are reluctant to concede defeat when a prospect tries to stop them with a positive "no." Instead they call into action their resourcefulness, their imagination, their persuasive power. They cash in on the turn-down. They develop sales in various ways, such as these:

(a) They follow up on all favorably qualified prospects whom they have failed to sell. They are challenged by being turned down by desirable prospects.

(b) They devise ways and means of recapturing the interest of prospects and to convince them of the benefits to be enjoyed by buying what the salesman has for sale.

(c) They load their follow-ups and call-backs with dynamic sales power.

(d) They search for new ideas and new uses which might prove beneficial to prospects who have turned them down.

(e) They build sales volume on ideas. Turn-downs stimulate their creative selling power.

HOW TO DEVISE AN EFFECTIVE FOLLOW-UP SYSTEM FOR CLOSING SALES

We now become tempters. Our objective is to present our product or service in its most favorable light. We dress it up. We give it glamour. We call attention to its alluring qualities. We stimulate desire for our product or service. We call this an effective follow-up system for attaining the ultimate objective in all sales efforts: To close more sales.

As many take-charge salesmen do, we might develop our follow-up system along these four lines:

1. *THE PLANNED CALL SYSTEM*
2. *THE REMINDER SYSTEM*
3. *THE INDIVIDUAL CARD SYSTEM*
4. *THE PHONE CALL SYSTEM*

Victor Hugo dropped a hint years ago about being on the right track. This is important to us as sales people. We systematically plan and follow up on contacts with qualified prospects. Hugo wrote: "He who every morning plans the transactions of the day, and follows out that plan, carries a thread that will guide him through the labyrinth of the most busy life." The four-point plan we have set forth places the emphasis on *SYSTEM* for effective selling. Take-charge salesmen find that a systematic, persuasive sales campaign usually yields profitable results.

An advertising salesman established a record in new sales made by systematically following through on all his calls. He commented:

> The secret of closing sales which you might have thought were lost is to improve communication. You may think that communication has been over-played in selling, but let us see if it has. My sales record has been built largely on better communication. In selling, regardless of what you sell, communication means to sell by enlightening others. I go out and you go out to tell prospective buyers about our lines and how effective and beneficial those lines can be in their lives. We get them worked up about what we have to sell. We get the message through to them and then they buy because, by effective communication, we have caused them to want to buy what we have to sell. This is what I call salesmanship by communication. Is there any other kind? The advertising copywriter sells goods and services by the same method except that he writes instead of communicating face-to-face. What he writes sells goods and services by the printed word or through the broadcast media. It's all based on a well-planned system and by a system of effective communication.

To devise an effective follow-up system for closing sales examine in depth the following four-point plan:

1. *OBJECTIVE*—To close a sale by the planned call system. (a) Determine why your prospect should be interested in what you have to sell. (b) Determine why you are justified in making the call on your prospect. (c) Determine how you propose to present your case. (d) Determine what your alternative proposal will be if your original idea fails to influence your prospect.
2. *OBJECTIVE*—To keep sales by the reminder system. (a)

Systematically keep a daily hour-by-hour calendar system for organizing yourself for effective selling. (b) Determine the best hours for scheduling calls on your various prospects. (c) Know enough about your prospects to determine the best time to approach them with a sales proposal. (d) Schedule vital calls at a time when Mr. Prospect will probably be in the most receptive mood.

3. *OBJECTIVE*—To close sales by the individual card system. (a) Set up an orderly card system that will be easily kept up to date, that is simple, that will be flexible. (b) Every day correlate dates on individual cards with dates on your daily calendar of calls. (c) Briefly and consistently note on individual cards any facts which may later contribute toward closing a sale.

4. *OBJECTIVE*—To close sales by using the telephone as a time-saver, an appointment-maker, and as a means of following through on leads. (a) Use persuasive approaches in phone calls to seek appointments with prospects. (b) Use the phone to follow up dubious leads to determine their validity. (c) Use the telephone to kindle interest in what you have to sell and also to detect time-wasting false alarm leads. (d) Make constructive and imaginative use of the telephone for stimulating indecisive prospects to act.

In-depth reviews of their follow-up systems have been productive for take-charge salesmen. For instance, an investment salesman declared that he sets aside thirty minutes before scheduled office time each day to go over his appointments for the day and his individual cards. "An early morning look at my prospects gets my thinking into constructive and creative channels for getting business that day," he said. "Those thirty minutes when I am alone often prove to be the most productive minutes of the day, measured in dollar-making ideas."

The sales manager of a chain of radio stations in medium-sized communities stirred up his sales staff one morning with this: "Any salesman worthy of his name should be able to present the average business man with at least one fresh, sales-promoting idea every time he calls." This sales manager inspired his staff to become take-charge sales people for their own welfare, sales-wise. His challenge to them was to devise and maintain an effective follow-up system for closing sales. The result: A noticeable gain in individual sales when individual follow-up systems were implemented by the sales staff.

HOW TO USE THE "RE-CAP" IN SALES PRESENTATIONS TO REVIVE INTEREST AND RENEW DESIRE

A leader in sales and marketing who was also directly engaged in the business of moving people and their belongings from place to place, was once quoted as saying: "Every successful man I have met had no idea of what a forty-hour week is." This man also voiced this principle: "Repeat sales are assured by cooperative effort of the sales and distribution staff." This principle is valuable when we take charge of sales situations having in mind the dual benefit technique. It also pinpoints the possibility of sales power in an effective follow-up system. Communication, cooperation, and persistence are involved in reviving and sustaining interest and in renewing desire for what we have to sell.

The crucial test of a salesman's ability comes at the moment when he senses that a prospect has lost interest in what he came in to sell. The dual benefit technique can, at that point, become a sales-saver. Moreover, the dual benefit technique can be mastered by most of us in selling. Some have called this technique "a shot in the arm." By using the "recap method" we can often revive interest in and renew desire for what we have to sell. In the "recap" we draw on the sales power in:

    (a) *RE-EMPHASIS*
    (b) *ENTICING EXAMPLES*
    (c) *SUGGESTIONS OF URGENCY*

At the root of the foregoing A,B,C's is the selling power in retelling about benefits to be enjoyed by a prospect. If he succumbs to that appeal then the salesman also benefits. Then we have cashed in on the dual benefit technique.

A sales consultant developed a notable personal sales record before becoming a consultant. Persuaded to reveal some of the successful methods he had used he said this:

"The basis for every successful sale is quite simple. This is it: (a) the ability to attract and hold the favorable attention of a prospect; (b) the ability to get favorable response from that prospect; (c) the ability to make it appear to be easy and desirable for that prospect to decide to buy what you have to sell."

As take-charge salesmen we can develop those skills which that sales expert has developed. Usually workable sales techniques are simple and they are motivating. For instance, hard facts about what we have to sell need not be cold facts. We can learn to dramatize those facts. When we do this we play upon the emotions of our prospects. When we succeed in stirring up their emotions we are on our way to success in selling.

In "recapping" we can spice our sales presentations with alluring, enticing examples of how someone else in a similar situation has profited or otherwise benefited by purchasing what we have for sale. "When I realized the effectiveness of that simple principle I began to rescue sales instead of losing them," said a highly productive security salesman. "It's simple to go over my whole presentation a second time with a prospect, but it pays off. As I go along I add glamour to the benefits. In repeating the main selling points I put extra power into *HOW* my prospect can benefit. I show him case after case of how persons he may know have benefited. This is the moment in sales situations when I have profited by having a thorough insight into the situations dominating the lives of my prospects. At this point I am persistent in going after a favorable decision. My main thrust is for two-way benefits—benefits for my prospect and benefits for myself."

HOW TO ARTFULLY AND EFFECTIVELY LEAVE A PROSPECT'S DOOR AJAR

We are now about to put our own resistance to the test. The situation arises when a prospect exhibits stubbornness so strongly that a sale appears to be lost. The supreme test, however, comes as we say goodbye to our obstinate prospect. What we say and how we say it may hold the key which may open the door to opportunity for us. Consider these simple ways of saying adieu to a balky prospect, thus leaving the door ajar:

1. Keep your "cool."
2. Express regret for misunderstanding, for failing to clearly show the prospect how he could benefit by buying what you have to sell.
3. Tactfully drop facts relating to what you have for sale, and to its connection with the prospect and his operation. Aim all this at reviving or maintaining the prospect's interest.

4. Give the prospect his head. Let him talk. Draw him into extended discussion. Let him hold the center of the stage. All this is aimed at reducing the size of the barrier.
5. Ask your prospect for names of friends who he thinks might benefit by what you have to sell. In effect, you are asking him to commit himself on the benefits possible through your product or service.
6. Depart with a smile. Leave with a gesture of good fellowship. Maintain a pleasant spirit of "too bad we couldn't work this out to your benefit."

The foregoing suggested ways of keeping doors ajar after a turndown require sales-sharp resourcefulness. This quality can be developed by self-examination wherein we can detect our strength and also our weaknesses.

A dynamic young salesman in the electronic office equipment field joined a group of salesmen at their club for lunch. He was unhappy when he arrived. "It jolts you," he said, "to lose a sale and then realize as you walk out how dumb you were in handling the best prospect of the morning. That happened to me today."

This dynamic young salesman had closed a door that he could have kept ajar. As he said, "I should be telling you how I shut a door instead of how I lost a sale. I am sure that in every sale I make I have said something that has sounded good to my prospect. If I will just take inventory of myself at the end of each day and find out what it was that I said or did that brought business for me I'd be a better salesman every day. In my daily soul searching I find that it is also profitable to find out what caused me to lose business and how I slammed doors shut that should have been kept open."

Sales seldom just happen. Sales in volume are the product of planning. They result from simple, understandable, convincing presentations. By keeping your "cool" in tight situations you equip yourself to leave doors ajar which might be slammed shut by tactless conduct.

The objective of keeping doors ajar: To sell more and more by the dual benefit technique.

Alexander Graham Bell, that Scottish-American scientist and inventor who came up with the telephone which became a boon to take-charge salesmen, once remarked: "When one door closes, another opens; but we often look so long and so regretfully upon the closed door that we do not see the one which has opened for us."

HOW THE ART OF TAKE-CHARGE SELLING CAN BEAT A SALES SLUMP

When we peek into the life and record of Thomas A. Edison we begin to believe that sales slumps and our state of mind are to some extent related. Edison left this thought with us to toy with when we come up with a barren day in selling:

"Results!" said Edison, "Why, man, I have gotten a lot of results. I know several thousand things that won't work."

As take-charge salesmen how many thousand ways do we know that won't work in combating our sales slumps?

How many ways do we know that *WILL* beat a sales slump?

The sales manager of a specialty house which has built a nation-wide clientele, included this in a bulletin to his sales force: "Sales slumps are beaten every day by some of our men who go in 'loaded for bear' to sell their prospects. Don't expect any prospect to *give* you an order. Our men develop sales records by selling, not by anticipating that anybody will give them anything."

A salesman who was writing more business than normal at the time his colleagues were complaining of a sales slump offered this explanation of how he did it: "Nobody rates a guy very high if he has the attitude that all he has to do is hold out his hand for business. I make it a point to go in prepared to sell and then I sell with all the steam I can get up. We win respect by bold selling."

The record indicates that relaxed salesmen are the first victims of a general slump in business in their areas. Those who promptly get aroused by a negative turn in the trade winds become the winners. They are the resourceful salesmen. They innovate. They have ideas about how their prospects can counteract a poor business trend and profit by it. They sell ideas that motivate potential buyers to buy. They talk about upward trends in business, never about a slump.

Sales people in all fields have ups and downs. Let us examine four areas to see if we can shed some light on how to beat a sales slump:

1. *RETAIL SALES PEOPLE*—The sales director of one large operation suggested this: "Too many in our stores are order-takers. They don't take this business seriously. Order-takers seldom succeed with us. We need and train resourceful, creative sales people and we have great opportunities for them—men and women who like people and who enjoy selling."

2. *ASSIGNED TERRITORY SALESMEN*—One of the resourceful men I know in the insurance field turns to cold-call
selling the minute he detects a sign of a let-down in his
production. "In cold-call selling I have learned to be a
closer," he said. "I return to cold calls frequently. This
sharpens my skills in the profitable phase of all selling—the
close."

3. *SPECIALTY SALESMEN*—in this area professional meets
professional in hot competition. Again, attitude shows up
clearly when you observe these competent, skillful take-
charge salesmen combat sales slumps in their lines. One of
these pros put it this way: "The best back-log I have discovered to support me against a worrisome drop in volume is
to vigorously go after two new accounts each week. If I
accomplish this I have added more than 100 accounts to my
list each year. That is a fair back-log against a slump. I
believe in thinking big. I also believe that little sales have
a way of swelling into big sales if I nourish the accounts."

4. *FREE-LANCE SALESMAN*—These are the unshackled
men and women who are beyond pressure from home-office
salesmanagers. How do they combat sales slumps? I asked
a woman in free-lance selling how she maintained volume.
She replied: "With ideas, with imagination, with work."

It is apparent that sales slumps can be and are beaten by take-
charge salesmen who *think big* and who *sell big*.

The Principle: Cultivate and maintain a winning frame of mind.

CHAPTER ELEVEN

HOW TO PERSUADE CUSTOMERS TO GO TO WORK FOR YOU

The objective of take-charge selling is to sell by capturing interest, by favorably impressing prospective buyers and by serving those buyers so well that they will spread the good word about you, and about your product or your service which you sell. Four points stand out in this objective. In case after case these four points have shown their selling power. Here is that quartet of sales-building points:

POINT NO. 1—Your approach. To open the door to a prospective buyer's sanctum and to immediately create within that prospective buyer's mind an attitude of "glad you came in," and to create an expectancy which by take-charge salesmanship you can exploit.

POINT NO. 2—Your bid for interest. To exploit the self-interest of your prospective buyer. He alone is the central figure in the selling process which you now have under way. You will remain at the con-

165

trol point to steer this sales presentation toward favorable decision and action by the prospective buyer. Your own self-interest must never cast a shadow over your presentation. It must be oriented toward glorifying the benefits and advantages for your prospective buyers.

POINT NO. 3—Your prospect becomes a customer. If point number one and point number two have been effectively executed, consummation of point number three should fall into place quite naturally. Your approach set the stage; your bid for interest revealed the purpose of your call; your summation heightened the prospect's desire for what you have for sale; your subtle, persuasive pressure assisted that prospect to make the decision to part with his (or her) money. You closed the sale.

POINT NO. 4—The customer becomes a booster. Dedicated, perceptive, far-seeing salesmen seldom permit one successful closing to close an avenue for more business. With them the closing is but the beginning of a pleasant, profitable association. By following through they become assured that the purchase turned out to be all that the customer had expected. They quickly clarify any point of misunderstanding. They become assured that delivery was made on schedule. They *resell* customers on their interest in customer welfare. They *resell* customers on their product. Their friendship campaign puts customers to work for them. Those customers become boosters. They spread the word. They expand the salesmen's lists of prospects. Those salesmen pave the way for continued growth in sales volume.

HOW TO WIN THE CONFIDENCE OF CUSTOMERS AND MAKE IT STICK

Plato, the Greek philosopher, evidently had a lot of sales sense. He said: "When men speak ill of you, live so nobody may believe them."

As a take-charge salesman you take command of sales situations by being a confidence-builder. You build confidence in yourself and also in others. The buyer for a large chain of department stores told me that he soon lost confidence in salesmen who made snide remarks about their competitors or who condemned a competing product.

A specialty salesman built up sales volume in a Seattle district where other salesmen had given up. Asked about the secret of his success, this take-charge salesman replied: "It's simple. The people here lost confidence in the other guys. For some reason, which they probably know best, those salesmen were one-call salesmen. When I came into this district I closed two or three accounts the first week. I made it a point to make them believe they were the most important customers I had. I called on them whenever I was in the area. Just a friendly call does a lot to keep customers working for you. Next door to every customer I have in this district, or somewhere near him, is another prospect for me whom that customer knows. If my customer boosts my stock it gets other doors half open for me before I call."

A salesman who travels three states selling uniforms direct to users maintains that his customers work willingly for him. "They get a great kick out of getting their friends to wear my brand of uniforms. I occasionally sweeten the way with a box of candy. Those girls, some gray-haired, boost my stock. They're on my team. I try to win favor with all my customers. If there is any complaint I adjust it fast . . . and I mean fast."

Winning the confidence of customers and making that confidence stick is the mark of most super-salesmen. A number of simple things often enter into confidence-building. Case records indicate that sales successes are associated with such qualities as these:

(a) *PUNCTUALITY*—Score one on this point for the salesman who is on time for appointments with prospective buyers. He's also on time to adjust a complaint. He's also on time to advise a customer so his purchase may prove to be the most beneficial to the customer.

(b) *HONESTY*—Score another point for being on the square. Honesty comes in many shades. Tom C. Clark, Supreme Court justice, looked at honesty in this way: "I'm convinced that every boy, in his heart, would rather steal sec-

ond base than an automobile." Square dealing salesmen
have a way of getting customers to work for them.

(c) *THOUGHTFULNESS*—This includes those unselfish
take-charge salesmen who remember. An insurance salesman I know keeps a calendar of birthdays of his clients,
of their wives, and of their children. About a week prior
to each birthday the one who is about to step into another
year gets a reminder that an insurance salesman hasn't
forgotten him (or her.) This stirs up thoughts about insurance. It becomes a conversation matter. It renews confidence in the salesman. The thoughtfulness of the salesman
who remembers dates that are important to prospects
becomes a subject of fireside chatting, back fence talk and
business conversation. Pleased clients recommend such
salesmen to their friends. Confidence in such salesmen
sticks. Their volume seems to keep climbing. This isn't
because they keep birthday calendars, but because they do
remember to take command of every sales situation to cause
it to yield its maximum potential or them.

A wholesale furniture salesman covers three western states. To
keep in touch with what is going on in the towns of his territory he
subscribes for a clipping service. This gives him a quick glance at
anything that affects furniture stores and furniture people in his
territory. The daughter of a much-desired prospect was injured in
an automobile accident. A clipping from the home-town newspaper
of that prospect informed the salesman of the girl's injury. He placed
a long-distance phone call to the father to inquire about his daughter's condition. This pleased the father and probably contributed
toward that salesman landing that much-desired account, for which
he had been plugging against stiff competition. Well-timed and
thoughtful phone calls often win the confidence of prospects in a way
that makes that confidence stick.

The confidence which we, as take-charge salesmen, try to win is
also known as trust. When we place ourselves in the prospect's place
we may well ask: "Can I trust this salesman?"

A famous Italian statesman who demonstrated persuasive political
salesmanship, made this comment on trusting one another: "The
man who trusts men will make fewer mistakes than he who distrusts
them."

HOW TO INCREASE SALES VOLUME
THROUGH THE ART OF SINCERE PRAISE

Jim was a book salesman. One night he attended a high school debate and was impressed by one student's performance. Her diction, her poise, her ability to dramatize with an easy delivery held the attention of her listeners. At the close of the meeting Jim made his way to the platform. He introduced himself to this girl. In sincerity he praised her. Her mother was near her daughter. With pride she shared the praise showered upon her daughter. The mother asked Jim if he was a teacher. "Of sorts," Jim replied. "I sell books." The mother beamed. "If you have anything that will be helpful to my daughter I'd like to have you call on me." Jim did. Jim sold the mother and the daughter on "something that would be helpful to the girl." He closed a substantial sale which encouraged Jim to continue to capitalize on the art of sincere praise.

A salesmanager in the publishing field repeatedly urged his staff to praise prospects who merited praise. He also warned his staff about flattery. Frequently he quoted Jean Paul Richter, who maintained that "it is easy to flatter, it is harder to praise."

A retail fur salesman developed business by attending college dramatic presentations and writing complimentary notes to praise-worthy women in the cast. He also capitalized on this sales-promoting idea by writing congratulatory letters to new officers elected in women's clubs and to women elected to office in other organizations.

Sincere praise can become a powerful selling tool, as many take-charge salesmen have discovered. When we engage in praise to encourage the worthy we are on the right track as sales-builders. In praising others both honesty and deception may be involved. In extending praise there are certain pitfalls which we should recognize. It was John Gay who wrote: "In one respect, indeed, our employment may be reckoned dishonest, because, like great statesmen, we encourage those who betray their friends."

A telephone call put through to congratulate a political figure on his victory and to praise him for conducting a clean, forthright campaign, opened doors of selling opportunity for the sales and public relations director of an expanding construction firm.

A personal call to tell the business executive how well his address to the chamber of commerce had been received thawed out an ice barrier that had stood between a radio time salesman and that business executive who was an influential buyer of spot radio commercials.

Dale Carnegie sold his formula on "How to Win Friends and Influence People" so well that the principles he espoused are still being taught for building sales volume. Included in Carnegie's techniques for handling people were these: "Begin with praise and honest appreciation," and "Praise the slightest improvement and praise every improvement. Be hearty in your approbation and lavish in your praise."

A salesman for a large chemical firm said he had noticed that asking a prospect for his opinion on a matter related to business usually pleased a prospect. It made the prospect feel important. In effect, it was recognition, which is a form of praise. At times it was flattery. Most important, however, it often opened doors to sales opportunities.

In the art of giving sincere praise the record clearly indicates that building sales volume can be hastened by honest and sincere praise. St. Augustine warned: "Falsely praising a person is lying." And, Norman Vincent Peale gave us a glimpse of our strength and our weakness in ambitious desires when he said: "The trouble with most of us is that we would rather be ruined by praise than saved by criticism."

The take-charge salesman, attempting to display his persuasive selling ability at home, might be encouraged in his purpose and also in his overall sales planning by this from the late Billy Sunday: "Try praising your wife, even if it frightens her at first."

The big objective of a take-charge salesman in creating good will is to enlist others in support of him and of his product. This is the skillful way of persuading others to go to work for you.

HOW TO QUALIFY AS A TRUSTED CONSULTANT FOR CUSTOMERS AND PROSPECTIVE CUSTOMERS AND PROFIT BY IT

One salesman who met the qualifications of a trusted consultant sold ranges—kitchen ranges. His territory was broken up insofar as a market for his cooking stoves was concerned. In some areas adequate electric power was unavailable. Some of his prospective customers were miles from the nearest transmission line. These people used coal and wood burning ranges. This salesman also sold those ranges. His whole territory was rough country. The winters usually were what the natives described as "hard winters." Snow kept them from their trading posts for days at a time. But, all of this discomfort added up to making that salesman a trusted consultant for merchants in the area. They phoned for his opinion on various problems. He became a kitchen range and marketing specialist. He became a trusted consultant on merchandising and stocking ranges. His reputation grew and grew. A merchant with a problem in that area just turned to that kitchen range salesman for advice because they had discovered that it paid to consult him. This built strong ties between that salesman and the merchants in his territory. His ability to dispense helpful advice persuaded customers to go to work for him. Being a trusted consultant built sales volume for that salesman.

In examining the record we find that there are certain sales-building principles which also qualify salesmen as trusted consultants for their customers and their prospective customers. Here we have a few of those sales-building qualifications:

1. *KNOWLEDGE*—A consultant must know whereof he speaks if he proposes to enlighten others. **The principle:** Know your market; know your product; know your people.
2. *SENSE OF DIRECTION*—A consultant requires a special quality which enables him to point out the way which a customer or prospective customer might follow for a profitable market venture. **The principle:** Develop perception. Capitalize on your market knowledge. Chart routes for greater output of your products through customers or prospective customers who can also profit by exploiting what you have to sell.
3. *CONFIDENCE*—This is a two-way quality: (a) You develop confidence in yourself by product knowledge and by serving others. (b) You develop self-confidence by attaining desirable and productive objectives. **The principle:** "Confidence is a thing not to be produced by compulsion. Men can't be forced into trust."—Daniel Webster.
4. *COMMUNICATION*—From master salesman to trusted consultant requires two-way communication. It requires listening as well as talking. Sales-wise, communication accounts for volume build-up and volume loss. We build confidence by communication. We improve our sense of direction

by improved communication. We gain knowledge, usable and expendable, by communication. We sell more when communication is good. **The principle:** To qualify as a trusted consultant, maintain open communication lines with customers and prospective customers. Objective: To become more productive as a take-charge salesman.

A jewelry salesman made the history of various gems his hobby. His knowledge of gems built confidence with jewelers and jewelry merchants. They sought him out to consult him. His hobby had qualified him as a trusted consultant on matters related to precious gems.

An advertising salesman had a flare for spectacular sales presentations. He developed business for his clients. He became known as a creative person with "limitless" ideas because his exploitations were profitable to his customers. As a result those exploitations were profitable to that salesman. His successes qualified him as a trusted consultant in sales promotion.

A securities salesman had an impressive personality. He caused customers and prospective customers to believe in him. His sincerity and his manner of approach, plus his knowledge of investment possibilities, qualified him as a trusted consultant. He rated high in sales production.

A wholesale salesman of paper products became a "walking encyclopedia" on papers, their printing qualities and their other uses. Printers consulted him on problems of color reproduction. His knowledge of paper qualified him as an expert, a trusted consultant in his field. Naturally sales volume came to him because, as a trusted consultant, that salesman also had persuasive power which moved paper in quantity.

HOW SPECIALIZING CAN LEAD TO GREATER SALES VOLUME IN TAKE-CHARGE SELLING

To break away from the routine of order-taking and become a take-charge salesman, specialization opens doors leading to new sales opportunities. Specializing has these advantages for you:

1. The salesman who becomes known as an expert, a specialist in one or more of the products he sells, has attained a certain status in the market place. This commands attention. This status rating adds credence to what he says. Consequently

     the specialist's sales presentations take on persuasive quali-
ties.

2. The salesman who has demonstrated that he is an expert,
a specialist, has thereby opened communication lines extending from himself to his customers and to his prospective
customers.

3. The salesman who has established himself as a specialist
inspires confidence in himself and in what he has for sale.

4. The salesman who, by his accomplishments, can boast of his
qualifications as a specialist doesn't boast of those attain-
ments. Instead of being boastful the salesman-specialist
demonstrates that he is knowledgeable, that he knows how
his prospect can efficiently and profitably use what he has
to sell. This is take-charge salesmanship of high order and
ultimately is profitable for the salesman.

A high school teacher was rated highly effective as an instructor
in mathematics. During a vacation he "tried his hand" at selling
books. He took to the road representing a book publishing house that
specialized in textbooks. The teacher-salesman made progress. His
sales of math textbooks attracted attention. It was evident that this
salesman was specializing without being aware of it. He never returned to the classroom. He continued to develop sales volume in
textbooks. He became, not only a specialist in his line, but a trusted
consultant among educators and buyers of textbooks. His reputation
caused customers to work for him.

Specialization in take-charge salesmanship often puts prospects at
ease because early in a sales presentation they detect that their spe-
cialist-salesman knows what he is talking about. He doesn't ramble.
He concentrates on how a product can benefit his prospect and shows
why this is true.

An automobile accessory salesman took the floor in a sales seminar and spoke on the profits made possible for salesmen by specializing in tire quality, tire care, and tire use, and also on tire merchandising. In the few minutes this salesman occupied the speaker's platform
he established himself among his colleagues as a tire specialist. His
sales record proved that his colleagues were right in so rating him.

In a fashion show in a highly-rated women's ready-to-wear shop
it was a man who was the voice in each modeled presentation. He
took immediate command of his captive audience and the sales

opportunity which this offered to him. In each garment that was modeled this salesman established in the minds of his listeners that "this man knows the fashion field." Moreover, he demonstrated that he knew fabrics and furs to their finest detail. He proved that he had a firm grasp of designing. He knew the sources of the startling creations that were being shown. He established himself as a specialist in what he was selling. At the conclusion of the fashion show there was a rush of customers and prospective customers to get to this salesman. It was apparent that he had qualified himself with those women as a trusted consultant. Already they were endorsing him; he had persuaded them to go to work for him.

Specialization leads to greater sales volume. It requires concentration. The salesman-specialist is thorough. He studies products in depth. He knows their capacity for benefiting users; their possibilities for yielding profits to buyers; their desirability for him to exploit as salable products.

The principle: As take-charge salesmen we specialize because we believe that what we sell is special. We believe that our products exceed or excel in some way which is usual or common. By this firm belief in what we have to sell we take command of sales situations, become take-charge salesmen in fact, and profit thereby.

HOW TO BE DIFFERENT AND RATE HIGHER AS A TAKE-CHARGE SALESMAN

Discussion at the Market Club self-service lunch room that day centered on a salesman who had reportedly come up with an unusual gain in business. The salesman in the limelight was a free-lancer—a specialty man who had been selling for several years. One of the men made this observation: "The temperature has been flirting with the hundred degree mark all this week and what happens? This guy goes out in the heat and makes a killing selling Christmas cards to business and professional men. He's different. Who'd think of Christmas cards in this July heat?"

Another question went the rounds of the men at the lunch counter: "Why did Pat Stern switch to making night calls?" The answer seemed simple to one of the men who knew Pat intimately. He explained: "Pat's sales took a sharp dip and he dug in to find out why. He discovered that he was losing time calling on buyers who were not in. So he tried cold canvassing at night and learned that a lot of business can be done in the quiet of the evening. Night workers in the supervisory and executive class seemed to be under less pressure than daytime workers in similar spots. Pat sells a variety of things for personal use and also for business use. Night calls have upped his sales and brought him out of a slump."

Someone broke in on the "gab" session to ask: "Did Pat give up day-time calls?" The answer: "Of course not. No salesman with Pat's experience would desert the customers and the prospects he has developed for day-time calls. His night calls amount to a different way of expanding his field of operation."

Every morning, six days a week, a housewife named Martha caught the bus on the corner and rode across town to work. She had prospects out there in her sales territory which she worked well as a cosmetic saleswoman. She rated as a "beauty consultant." One of her neighbor's was in Martha's bridge club. One night she remarked: "It must be fascinating to meet new people every day." This gave Martha an idea. She decided to take a new approach to her work. Instead of riding across town in pursuit of customers she called on her neighbors. She had called on them many times but this time it was different. She called to sell to them and to establish them as her customers, and to establish herself with them as a "beauty consultant."

A doctor told a hard-driving salesman in the insurance business to cut down on long drives and concentrate his efforts in a smaller area. "You're burning yourself out," warned the doctor. This salesman began developing business within walking distance of his office. He used the telephone more effectively, thus saving time and conserving his energy. Soon he became aware of how much time and energy had been wasted in non-productive activity, such as long drives without a fixed sales objective. Being different paid off for this salesman.

Among the customers an office supply salesman served the coffee-break chatter was about the change that had come over that salesman. "He's different," a number of his customers contended. He had been a "hurry away" salesman. When he had written an order and the buyer had initialed it that salesman had seldom taken a minute to exchange pleasantries before departing. All that had changed and this made him a subject of conversation among those he served. He was taking time to become part of the lives of his customers. They like the change. "He's a different guy," they were saying. "We enjoy having him come in." Being different was also showing up on that salesman's reports. He was selling more by being different and getting closer to those he served. By being different in a way that gave him a more favorable image he increased his sales volume. He became, in fact, a take-charge salesman.

To be different is relatively simple. Most of the top flight salesmen are different in many ways. But, it isn't complicated to keep in mind a prospect who operates next door to you. It's not difficult to be different by making two or three extra calls while your car is still parked instead of pulling out and driving two or three blocks and there hunting for another parking place. It's not too complicated to be different by looking and planning ahead instead of operating in a routine seasonal pattern. Christmas business can be developed in the hottest day of summer, and to talk about Christmas in July has a different way of capturing a buyer's attention. It's not complicated to be different in your telephone attitude. You can be different and you can develop your technique of building good will by following through on sales by a friendly sales-promoting phone call. A telephone is a great selling tool, especially with those who have learned the art of being different in telephone conversation. They find that a phone call can often persuade a customer to go to work for them, directly or indirectly.

HOW WOMEN RATE AS TAKE-CHARGE SALES PEOPLE

Women have carved out for themselves a place in selling which places them in top rating among take-charge sales people.

Few things please a woman more than being able to say to her husband, "I told you so!" In one such instance the wife went a step farther. She said: "I'll show you how to sell." And she did.

Several times that wife had suggested to her husband that he was missing too many sales in covering his territory. He sold advertising specialties, including executive gifts and holiday greeting cards. Talk failed to convince him that more volume was available. To clinch her case his wife took on a line of greeting cards in competition with the lines he carried. The upshot was that she was soon crowding her husband's total in volume sales simply by take-charge salesmanship in greeting cards alone. She sold a wholesale line to dealers for resale. She also sold exclusive Christmas and New Year cards to business executives, professional men and women, and to companies for distribution to employees. Her record reveals that she was doing more than selling greeting cards. She was selling ideas for productive use of greeting cards. Much of her business resulted from referrals by customers working for her.

I recall a salesman and a saleswoman who were in direct competition for business among nurses and other hospital employees. The "no soliciting" signs in elevators, in the lobby and in the waiting rooms stopped the salesman, but not the saleswoman. Both sold similar lines. They handled beauty aids plus easy-on-the-feet shoes, and also uniforms. The resourceful saleswoman went to the coffee shop, checked on coffee-break times and patronized the coffee shop at various coffee-break hours. She was a good "mixer." By resourcefulness and by establishing a favorable relationship with the hospital personnel she soon had her appointment book so crowded that she had little time for coffee-breaks herself. More and more pleased customers were recommending her products to others.

Another of the resourceful sales people I have known was a woman. She closed insurance sales where men failed to get through the doors. She had sold herself so well that customers voluntarily went to work for her just to see that their friends "bought the right kind of protection."

A young widow was swept off her financial feet by the collapse of the business her husband had established. This attractive and resourceful widow went on and developed a business for herself, using the account records in her husband's now defunct furniture business as her foundation. She went away for special study, after which she set up shop as an "interior decorator consultant." She did exceptionally well. A salesman who had worked for her husband said, "I was sure you intended to go into the furniture business." She smiled as she replied, "I did, except this time I sell what furniture can do for a home and for better living. If you and the other clerks in the store had sold ideas about using furniture instead of peddling tables and chairs the store might still be in operation. You see, my customers are delighted with the help I give them in furnishing their homes and they send their friends to me. I see no end to the growth of my business."

The principle: Never underestimate the resourcefulness and persuasive sales power of a woman.

HOW THE COMMAND PRINCIPLE WORKS
IN TAKE-CHARGE SELLING

Two questions arise when we explore the command principle in selling a product or a service: (a) Will it sell? (b) How can it best be sold?"

The command principle in selling is more than a catch-phrase. It has substance. We can test the command principle in selling in many areas. The command principle gives muscle to take-charge selling. A salesman activates the command principle when he is challenged by stiff sales resistance. He breaks down that resistance by rising to take command of the sales situation.

Salesmen who overcome objections to buying and convert objections into reasons for buying place themselves in command of those sales situations. They convert objections into selling points, brush aside opposition, and move ahead to close the sale. They profit by the command principle in take-charge selling.

Salesmen who welcome stiff competition as a challenge to their ability to sell and meet such competition head-on are employing the command principle in selling.

By adopting the command principle in selling you, too, can sell more and profit more as a take-charge salesman. Other salesmen in a multitude of lines are doing this. Here are 10 points which are involved in the command principle in take-charge selling. Check these 10 points now. Check them against your own sales performance:

1. *ENTHUSIASM*—How do you rate yourself on this point? The command principle in selling is based on enthusiasm. A real estate salesman declares that the command principle worked at peak capacity for him. When he combined product enthusiasm with eagerness to explore new areas for increasing sales his sales volume went up. He said his interest in people and how he could serve them fed his enthusiasm for work.

2. *ORGANIZATION*—The command principle is based on concentrated action. A salesman representing a notable home-study school clinches his selling points with facts and by a well-organized presentation. In this way he activates the command principle in take-charge selling.

3. *HONESTY*—We are digging deeper now. Honesty is the

rich kernel within the hard shell of take-charge selling. Its greatest effect is noted in the command principle in selling. A direct-to-consumer roofing salesman said honesty builds confidence in customers. He said that honesty creates a favorable image of the salesman and this alone can turn a tide of business toward him. This salesman's viewpoint seems to be in accord with Horace Greeley, who said: "The darkest hour in any man's life is when he sits down to plan how to get money without earning it."

4. *IMAGINATION*—A printing salesman specializing in letterhead creations demonstrated that the creative spirit, applied to salesmanship, invigorates sales presentations. His sales technique stimulated his self-confidence and shed a persuasive light on the impressive stationery display which he used in his presentations. He was a take-charge salesman who took command of sales situations by imaginative selling.

5. *PRODUCT KNOWLEDGE*—Armed with "know how" about what he had for sale a specialty food products salesman seized command of his sales situations. He radiated self-assurance that was convincing. He showed that he had a thorough knowledge of what he had for sale. He maintained command of sales situations. His attitude kept him out of hot water and led him into the calm waters of sales growth.

6. *SHOWMANSHIP*—The "how" element in the command principle of selling builds sales volume. An automobile salesman built sales volume by convincing showmanship. On a giant display board he graphically showed facts and figures to convince his prospects that the car he had for sale was the right car for them to buy.

7. *CONVICTION*—In each step of the selling process conviction leads to closing sales. The command principle in selling is based on the concept that total knowledge of your product can persuade prospects to believe in you and in your product. This can be achieved by imaginative presentations, by persuasive demonstrations, by your own strong testimony of why you believe in the product you are exploiting. We call this conviction. To sell we must achieve conviction. We must strive to convince our prospects that

it is to their benefit to buy. We do this by remaining firmly in command of each sales situation all the way from the approach to the moment of closing.

8. *COURTESY*—A polite salesman in the jewelry field maintained that courtesy and decency have a softening, persuasive effect in selling. That jewelry salesman, by comfortable courteousness, took immediate command of sales situations and profited by it. Close observation disclosed how persuasive courtesy can become in selling. With that jewelry salesman it paid high dividends, as his sales record showed.

9. *DESIRE TO SERVE*—The command principle works best in take-charge selling when there is a well-motivated desire to serve prospects and customers. An insurance salesman points out that contact with those he has sold keeps them advised of new "opportunities" in insurance, and, as a result, his sales continue to climb. He is an "in command" take-charge salesman. When he closes a sale that customer goes on that salesman's prospect list. He remains in command by never losing contact with a customer.

10. *PERSISTENCE*—For success in take-charge salesmanship note this from Elbert Hubbard, publisher and author: "A little more persistence, a little more effort, and what seemed hopeless failure may turn to glorious success." Persistence has been the secret of many outstanding successes in selling. The command principle becomes a dynamic factor in take-charge selling when it is combined with persistence.

CHAPTER TWELVE

HOW TO BRING HOME UNDREAMED OF WEALTH WITH TENSION-FREE COMMAND SELLING

At the foot of a salesman's rainbow there is a pot of gold. That pot is filled by applying the principles of take-charge selling. Those principles have been tested. They produce sales. You can master those principles with the following results:

(a) Enjoy maximum yield from your selling effort by constructive, imaginative planning.
(b) Reduce tension and thereby build greater sales volume.
(c) Seize and maintain control of every sales situation, thereby overcoming obstacles which have threatened to drain your pot of gold.

Domination is the key to selling power. Dominate each sales situation. Salesmen who run scared sell little. Arrogant salesmen and overbearing salesmen sell little. The areas in which high yields in sales are registered are relatively smooth. These are the areas in which persuasive salesmen are in the saddle. Persuasive salesmen are confident. They are sure of the value of their products. They know how their products can be used with profit to users. They dramatize. They animate the uses to which their products can be put. They show how their products can contribute to the lives of those to whom they propose to sell their products.

Sales power gains in strength when salesmen become take-charge salesmen in fact. You, too, can enjoy the fruits of self-organization by seizing control of your life and thereby skyrocketing your income.

An investment sales counselor found a relatively simple way to gain the time necessary to more effectively develop prospective clients. He freed himself of an overload of paperwork. First he seized control of himself and refused to allow paperwork to "bug" him. Then he disposed of necessary paperwork with efficient, productive action. By selective elimination he got the least important matters out of the way, giving top priority to vital matters.

A drug salesman broke down the causes of some of his most annoying sales situations. To his dismay he discovered that even in the most unpleasant encounters sales tips were hidden. By uncovering those tips and recognizing the worth in them he was able to capitalize on them.

A sales executive in a far-flung merchandising operation, producing and selling a variety of products, made this observation: "Salesmen who are on their toes in today's highly competitive market must understand that all the selling genius and all the sales promotion in the world will not sustain sales volume of an unneeded product. Case histories prove conclusively that salesmen who know their products, who know their uses, and who know how others can benefit by buying and using their products are the stars in the drama of creating sales power and closing sales."

Try to recall the details of your last sale. It probably had within it at least one secret of success in closing sales. If you dig deeply into the case you probably will uncover a hidden factor which made it possible for you to close a sale that had been difficult to bring to a head.

To seize control of your life in selling and to build sales volume by tension-free, take-charge selling, the following seven keys to success in selling have been tested and have opened doors to untapped reservoirs of sales opportunities:

1. *LOVE THOSE PRODUCTS*—Generate interest in people.
2. *HAVE FUN WORKING*—Enjoy your work. Selling successes are not built on rigid forty-hours-a-week schedules.
3. *TAKE PRIDE IN ACCOMPLISHMENT*—"It's neat! I worked out that plan myself! It sold!" With that attitude of excitement in accomplishment sales power is developed.
4. *KNOW YOUR PRODUCT*—Get excited over what you are selling. Get better acquainted with your product. Study, experiment, innovate.
5. *"I'D RATHER SELL THAN . . ."*—How strong is your desire to sell? What would you rather do than sell? Top-rated take-charge salesmen have a ready answer for that question.
6. *"MAN, DO I FEEL GREAT TODAY!"*—Nothing, but nothing, contributes so much to dynamic selling as a body and mind in tune, at the peak of good health.
7. *BECOME A MINUTE-MISER*—Sales geniuses dodge time-wasting. They are stingy with their minutes.

FIVE KEYS TO RELEASE YOUR SELLING POWER

A "score board" which hung in a sales manager's office contained one significant thing about salesmen and salesmanship. All territories outlined on that scoreboard had these things in common: (a) each of those territories had top-flight producers piling up sales volume; (b) each of those territories had its share of the "no more than quota" men; (c) each of those territories had its share of borderline and mediocre men.

I asked about some of those men. The sales manager pointed out that some of the top-flight men had been shifted from time to time in an effort to develop business in low-production areas. Those top-flight men, he said, rarely let him down. They became top-flight men by becoming top producers wherever they were assigned. He went on to tell about some of the borderline men. He had shifted them from time to time in an effort to develop their sales power. But, there was no change in their production. The sales manager explained: "Unfortunately mediocre men fail to respond to challenges. They turn in a passable volume and there they stop. The difference between them and our top-rated men is that the top producers drive on to top yesterday's record. The mediocre men write a few sales and that satisfies their appetite."

That sales manager was striving to release all of the selling power in his staff. In shifting men into new pastures he was presenting fresh challenges to those men—new opportunities to make more money and to raise their status in the market place.

Five keys seem to unlock many chambers where dynamic sales power is often locked up. A survey of salesmen specializing in a wide variety of products revealed that the following five keys had the greatest respect among top-rated salesmen:

1. *SIMPLIFY IT*
2. *CLARIFY IT*
3. *DRAMATIZE IT*
4. *BELIEVE IN IT*
5. *DEMONSTRATE IT*

A buyer in a large department store made this point on simplification in selling. He said:

> Usually ı can detect a novice in the business by the way he gushes forth with big words and extravagant, involved statements. The men calling on us who write most of the business in my workshop present their proposals in simple language. They simplify a new product. They simplify its uses. They simplify the whole reason for me to buy. They explain to me how I can resell with profit what they have to sell to me. It's that simple.

An insurance salesman told me that the most difficult thing about selling insurance is to make its benefits clear to the prospect. If those benefits are not made clear, he said, the prospect may buy with a wrong impression of what he has bought. As a result, he explained, that man is a potential "policy dropper." He isn't really sold, he said, until you clarify the problem for him.

A toy salesman had a faculty for dramatizing what he sold. At one time he pulled a clown-like toy through a crowded but slow-buying mass of shoppers. This salesman's dramatization of a mechanical toy started people buying. Business also picked up for the salesman. He sold toys in volume to that store by his colorful presentation which gave proof of his product's potential value to the dealer.

Belief rates a ring-side seat in the sales arena. One veteran wholesale shoe salesman told this to a young man going out on his first trip into the territory: "Study those shoes," the veteran salesman told the younger man. "Get your feet into them. Feel the comfort in those shoes. Then work yourself up until you believe so strongly in those shoes that no other shoe quite measures up to your expectations. That," the veteran salesman concluded, "is the secret of selling anything. You've just got to believe if you hope to get others to believe in what you have to sell."

One three-letter word has dynamic selling power. The word is: *HOW.* When you succeed in demonstrating *HOW* your product can benefit a prospect you have a buyer, if your presentation has been convincing. Smart automobile salesmen demonstrate their cars. TV salesmen demonstrate *HOW* superior their product is in color reception. The top-rated woman in a fashion shop effectively *SHOWS HOW* a $1,000 coat will enhance the prestige and attractiveness of her prospective female buyer. Cutlery, home appliances, furniture, snowmobiles, and many other products are sold by demonstration. *HOW* these products perform and *HOW* they can add to the profits, or to the pleasures, or to the comfort, or to the overall benefit of prospective buyers sells those products. When demonstration becomes so believable, so convincing that it wins over a prospect's natural resistance against buying a sale results. Behind that sort of conviction on the part of the buyer is the faith and belief of the salesman in what he has for sale. The five keys, which have been tested in the market place—the laboratory of selling—actually open doors to greater sales volume and to higher earnings for the salesman. Those five keys can release your selling power.

HOW TO SYSTEMATIZE SELLING BY TAKE-CHARGE METHODS

Someone has said there can be no systematic way to sell goods or services. However, knowingly or unknowingly, systematic selling by take-charge methods is producing sales in virtually every field in which goods are moved from the production line to consumers.

To systematize means that we so order our sales efforts that we aim to close the books each day with a gain in profitable volume. There is a systematic way to do this. The principle is quite simple: Sell more by more orderly and more persuasive take-charge salesmanship.

How, then, do we go about systematizing our work so we can come up with a workable, productive method? Let us consider the following four steps for better organization in our take-charge selling:

1. *SYSTEMATIZE PROSPECTING*
2. *SYSTEMATIZE PLANNING*
3. *SYSTEMATIZE EXPENDITURE OF TIME*
4. *SYSTEMATIZE SALES PRESENTATIONS*

Some salesmen refer to prospecting as "beating the bushes." This describes the first and vital step in salesmanship. We assume that prospects are in hiding behind every bush in our territory. We systematically proceed to "beat those bushes" to get at those prospective buyers. It would be comparatively easy to "flush out" prospects in this way if prospects actually were in hiding. But, they are not. As one dynamic salesman in the investment field said: "I find good prospects in the darnedest places. By chance I ran into one the other day when my car stalled on a country road. A big fellow, dressed in coveralls, came along and got me under way. In expressing my gratitude to him I learned from his remarks that I have a live one and I followed up on this accidental acquainceship. The result: Several sales and a well-established client-salesman relationship."

Planning plays a vital role in every salesman's life. Those who systematize their planning profit most. As Victor Hugo reminded us: "He who every morning plans the transactions of the day, and follows out that plan, carries a thread that will guide him through the labyrinth of the most busy life."

Hugo also left this thought on the expenditure of time, by which many take-charge salesmen have profited: "The orderly management of time is like a ray of light which darts itself through all his occupations. But, where no plan is laid, where the disposal of time is surrendered merely to the chance of incidents, all things lie huddled together in one chaos."

A man who amassed a fortune in the food industry attributes his success to systematizing. "I systematized my selling when I first began calling on store operators as a wholesale food specialty salesman. I found out that I could cover more ground and sell more if I planned my calls in advance, used my allotted time to the most productive advantage, and worked out a method of sales presentation that had self-interest appeal for my prospects. Much of my success has been the result of never relaxing in my search for prospects."

A farm equipment salesman pointed out that salesmen in most lines can climb ladders to higher sales volume by cooperating with and winning the cooperation of all departments in the firm. This salesman systematized his selling program by keeping in touch with the credit department, the shipping department, the billing department and the advertising department. When these departments become aware of sales problems and how they can either boost or knock down sales a new and constructive spirit develops to benefit, not only the salesmen, but the whole firm in general. By the same token, the salesman who is in close touch with customers in his territory can often provide valuable information to assist other departments.

A specialty salesman who covered a large territory in the western states chalked up consistent gains in sales. When something new was added to his widely varied line he wrote personal notes to his customer-friends in his territory, indicating an interest in their welfare. "Of course," he said, "the factory gets out colorful folders, brochures and what-nots. That's great, but I have found additional selling power in a personal note, in person-to-person closeness, in the hand shake, or in a phone call. My system is to get as close to the source of business as I can. My purpose all day long is to sell!"

HOW TO SEIZE CONTROL WHEN YOU RAISE THE CURTAIN FOR YOUR PRESENTATION

The salesman with his eye on a target of capturing new accounts has a fight on his hands to increase his sales volume. Other eager salesmen are going to beat paths to the doors of his prospects as well as to his established customers. Those who come out victorious in this skirmish for business are those who demonstrate that they are skillful, knowledgeable sales strategists. This isn't too complicated. Take-charge salesmen representing virtually every line on the market battlefront emerge from the fray with few wounds and often with many victory decorations.

Let us set it up this way: (a) define the target for today; (b) select prospects known for their attitude of stiff sales resistance; (c) define and establish your objective, which is to beat down their sales resistance and to sell to them; (d) work out your strategy to attain your objective. Plan your attack in a step-by-step advance to overcome all resistance and to emerge with sales.

STEP No. 1—You adopt a sound principle of attack. You arm yourself with sales weapons in order to conquer. You decide to launch an initial blow with maximum selling power to throw your prospects off balance before they can get their sales-resisting artillery into action.

STEP No. 2.—You overload yourself with product facts. You fire these persuasive facts at your prospects to show your prospects how your product can yield benefits to those who activate it in their business or in their lives. You fortify yourself with fact ammunition about quality, about utility, about desirability, about durability, about adaptability of your product. All this is planned to convince those who buy your product that they can benefit by it.

STEP No. 3.—You clarify and dramatize. You reiterate selling points which strike directly at the prospect's self-interest. You return to these points as frequently as necessary to achieve maximum impact. Your prospect may question or challenge some point you have made. This opens the door for strengthening your sales position. By asking questions or by challenging you your prospect discloses that he is interested, that he can be sold. Strive to be understood. Strive to hold your prospect's interest. The most dramatic sales presentation is the one that directly affects the prospect, that appeals to his welfare, and that stirs him to do something about it.

STEP No. 4.—You retain command of the sales situation during each step of your presentation by averting any attempt of your prospect to take over. You do this by holding to the position that you are there to sell something to him that is for his benefit. You hammer away at his self-interest. You appeal to the selfish man within him. By being sincere and convincing in this your prospect goes along with you. In substance, that is persuasive, take-charge salesmanship. That is how to be a take-charge salesman.

Probably the greatest asset a take-charge salesman can have is to be interesting. Next on the list of assets is a personal enthusiasm for work, for people, and for the product to be sold. The side-show barkers who sold their wares at the gateway to circuses exercised strong persuasiveness. Most of these masters of mass appeal crushed sales resistance by smothering it with enthusiasm.

The first few minutes in the presence of a prospect are vital in the sales process. As Jim Marx, who rated high in door-to-door selling, said: "When my prospect opens the door I say something to capture immediate attention. This 'something' must create desire or arouse curiosity or otherwise appeal to the self-interest of the prospect, or it falls flat. It must go beyond attracting attention to me. I am there to sell, not to perform as an actor. The greatest interest-promoting factor in a product is how it can benefit the prospective buyer. I go right to work on developing that point when a prospect opens the door for me."

A salesman in a man's clothing store played heavily on the sex-appeal angle. I overheard this salesman making this sort of pitch: "Wives who come in here with their husbands go wild over this new look in men's jackets." There he got women into the picture. Through them he played on male pride, on male vanity, and on a man's desire to present a good appearance. That salesman wasn't dull. Not for a precious selling moment. He seized control at the beginning of his presentation and never lost his grip on the sales situation.

HOW TO INDUCE PROSPECTS TO PARTICIPATE IN AND STRENGTHEN YOUR SALES PRESENTATION

An appliance salesman stood in front of a new model freezer-refrigerator which was being introduced to the market. Newspaper, magazine and TV promotion had created consumer interest in this new development in household appliances. The salesman whom I was observing was not alone. Two women were seated in front of him. He stood between them and the appliance he was selling. He spoke to them in glowing terms about the appliance but he blocked part of their view of it. When he had completed his pitch the women strolled away, chattering. Minutes later that salesman was relieved by another salesman. The two women returned. The second salesman invited them to examine all the features of the freezer-refrigerator. They pried into every corner of it. They asked questions. They examined the compartments and the shelves. They were involved in the sales process. Participation heightened their interest. The result: The two sisters who lived together bought that appliance. The second salesman had strengthened his sales presentation by inviting his prospects to participate, to get involved.

An automobile salesman who has become noted for sales power

in moving luxury cars declared at a sales seminar: "Until you get a prospect behind the wheel and a woman seated beside him you haven't even begun to sell a car in my class." That salesman builds volume by prospect participation and involvement in the selling process.

The manager of an exclusive jewelry shop makes this point: "Sales people who attempt to sell gems, rings, and other items in our line by keeping these items under glass and simply pointing to them are usually low in total sales. The sales people who get a ring on a prospect's finger, a wrist watch on a prospect's wrist, or a necklace around the neck of a woman, and get her before a mirror to glorify her and the jewelry, are the sales people who keep our sales volume climbing."

The salesman for a leading chain saw producer went deep into the timber country with a stock of late model chain saws in his pickup truck. He returned with an empty truck because he put those chain saws in the hands of timber men who admired fine tools and what such tools could do for them. Those rugged men were eager to participate in that salesman's presentation. By inducing prospects to participate in demonstrations of how they could do a better job easier with his product that take-charge salesman sold chain saws.

The principle: Get likely prospects into the act. Let them see, feel and use your product. Relate your product to those to whom you propose to sell it.

HOW TO USE PRICE AND QUALITY COMPARISONS FOR SALES POWER

A volume-building salesman in home furnishings made this point as we discussed methods of using comparisons of price and quality:

> To give sales power to such comparisons I have found that I have to convince my prospects that my price or the quality of my product will do something special for the prospect. I make headway when I succeed in exposing the desires that sway the prospect's thinking. I make headway when I can show the prospect that there is something worthwhile in my proposal, something in it for the benefit of the prospect.

Salesmen in various fields are quick to admit that there is selling power in comparisons of price and quality. Among those who consistently write volume business are the staunch advocates of slanting any comparative appeal toward what it will do or can do for the prospect. An automobile salesman aptly called the price-quality comparison a "more for the money pitch." He maintained that "more for the money" has sales power when it is made convincingly.

There are three areas in which we frequently notice the price-quality comparison used in selling. The basic theme of the sales appeal in these areas is "super quality at an economy price." This is a challenging idea for a prospect. Take-charge salesmen can exploit this theme by working their sales presentations toward showing what there is in their proposals for their prospects. For instance:

UP-GRADED AUTOMOBILES are sold on prestige appeal. They are sold on better performance appeal. They are sold on better mileage and economy appeal. They are sold on giving the buyer more for his money and by identifying all of those benefits with the prospect, and by supplying data to support all of his claims.

UP-GRADED CLOTHING is sold in volume to men and to women by such challenging appeals as these: "Imagine what this can do for you. . . . Your friends will envy you when you step out in this outfit. . . . Think of how good you will feel in one of these superbly-tailored garments. . . . These clothes are growing in demand in the most fashion-conscious markets. . . . This line will take the lead in your market here and can increase your total volume as it has for hundreds of other dealers."

UP-GRADED HOMES are sold on multi-benefit proposals. Prestige, comfort, convenience, low maintenance cost, more for the money—all these figure in building up sales power to sell homes. Astute real estate salesmen show prospects how easy it can be for them to move up to more prestigious living for "so little more." By facts and figures and well-developed sales presentations they convince the doubtful that they can enjoy "so much more" comfort by paying "so little more." When they have a qualified prospect, fiscally sound, they move in for the close by hammering away on the theme of "the best costs only a few dollars more."

Regardless of the product or the service you may be selling you can put sales power into price and quality comparisons by keeping the consumer viewpoint in mind. The better price, the more attractive deal, the quality and desirability of a product or the productivity of a service constitute the ingredients of sales power for what you have to sell. By presenting it appealingly to your prospect as something desirable for him (or her) you show and try to convince your prospect how your product or your service can or will enable him (or her) to profit in some way by having it; how it will yield comfort, beauty, pride, fun, prestige, or how it can fatten his (or her) bank account. In this way you can build a dynamic sales appeal to combat sales resistance.

Even a product such as a detergent is sold on a price-quality comparison basis. The pitch may vary but essentially this is what the prospect is told, and it does sell: "In the long run the cost is lower. Our detergent requires less to do a good job and it does clean better."

The principle: Whenever we make a price-quality comparison we show how the prospect can benefit most by using our product or our service. We make it convincing, appealing, and persuasive.

HOW TO SUCCEED THROUGH FAITH AND COURAGE IN TAKE-CHARGE SELLING

A former president of Rotary International, the late Richard L. Evans, who displayed the same power of persuasiveness which can carry salesmen up to greatness, once remarked: "We must preserve the incentive to succeed and the right to fail."

In take-charge selling success seems to attend those who have faith in (a) themselves; (b) in their product; (c) in their prospects. Those who have such faith also seem to draw from that faith the personal courage which spurs them on to exceed the accomplishments of yesterday and to envision greater accomplishments for tomorrow.

A syndicate salesman was constantly going places to call on editors and publishers, trying to persuade them to "take on" the works of writers, artists and photographers. He was selling a circulation-building product. He firmly believed that the features he sold had reader appeal, that they would attract new readers to publications and that they would also hold readers already on the lists of subscribers. This salesman had faith in his product. He believed that what he sold could benefit those who bought it and also the readers who were attracted to the publications to which he sold his syndicated features. In addition to the abiding faith that salesman had in his product and in his own ability to "put it over," he was steamed up with the courage that builds sales volume.

Case records in various lines reveal that emotions play a tremendous role in selling. As take-charge salesmen we profit by stimulating desire in others for what we have to sell. We do this by playing on the emotions of our prospects. We also strive to develop in our prospects a certain amount of faith in what we have to sell. When that faith becomes strong enough we achieve conviction, and then the way is clear for closing the sale. Enthusiasm, too, may be classified as an emotional effect which take-charge salesmen have found to be exceedingly profitable for them. Successful salesmen are finding that work and achievement feed and energize enthusiasm. Case records provide evidence that enthusiasm is a sales-builder.

Let us switch from the positive emotions we have discussed and examine three negative emotions. They are sales-killers. They are: (a) fear; (b) greed; (c) distrust. The perceptive take-charge salesman recognizes this trio as destroyers and gives them the cold shoulder. Doing this the take-charge salesman demonstrates his strength. He convinces himself that sales volume can be built on the positives, on faith, courage and enthusiasm. He moves on to stimulate desire for what he sells. He personally profits by faith and courage.

HOW TO MAKE CLOSING EASIER AND MORE EFFECTIVE

At a period when men were being layed off due to a temporary slump in the building industry the area representative for a nationally recognized home-study school took charge of the sales possibilities in this local situation and achieved a notable sales record. The secret of his success was the way he planned his selling campaign. By thorough planning he made closing easier and more effective. This was his five-point plan:

1. *IN-DEPTH PROSPECTING*
2. *PERSUASIVE, DESIRE-BUILDING APPROACHES*
3. *DRAMATIC, MOTIVATING PRESENTATIONS*
4. *NO-GAP FOLLOW THROUGH*
5. *SIMPLIFYING THE PROSPECT'S PROBLEM*

The home-study salesman was working against a negative situation but he found a way to cash in on it. He dug out the "how it can be done" angles and took charge of them. In-depth prospecting enabled him to understand his prospects and their personal problems and their ambitions. By imaginative planning he was able to present to his prospects motivating facts about the possibilities for self-improvement by home study. The combination of in-depth prospecting, desire-building approaches and motivating presentations resulted in easier closing of sales.

A salesman for a printing machinery manufacturer made sales records by finding out about the needs or probable needs of prospective buyers for his product.

A salesman for an office supply house built sales volume by prospecting in depth even with his established accounts. "I'm always prospecting," he explained. "I observe, I inquire, I listen and thereby I learn how what I have to sell can be profitably used by those to whom I try to sell. The secret of easy closing and more effective closing is better prospecting plus more convincing sales presentations."

An advertising specialty salesman who had a highly favorable closing record created desire for what he had to sell by what he called "mass persuasion." One gimmick he used effectively was to spill a large quantity of ball point pens of various colors and designs on the desk of a prospect. "Which of these pens would you say would do the best job in promoting your business?" he would ask. Any response from the prospect opened the door for the salesman to expand on his presentation. This proved to be a sales producer.

Speaking at a sales seminar a securities salesman told his colleagues about how he came up from a low production man to a high producer.

> I discovered that the bulldog grip had great sales potential. I noticed that salesmen who were the most prosperous were persistent. When they got hold of a live one they stayed with him. They used every stratagem in the book to hold that prospect's favorable attention. Ultimately they planted the seeds of desire and nourished them so well that they sprouted and yielded sales in volume.

Most of the effective closers I have known have been enthusiastic sales people. A woman who developed many major accounts for an advertising agency succeeded because she was interesting, enthusiastic, persistent and very knowledgeable about what advertising could do as a selling force. She knew her line. She was sure that the agency she represented could develop business for her prospects. She maintained a "bulldog grip" on a live prospect. She let it be known that she was there to show her prospect that there were greener pastures that could, with advertising know-how, be seeded and cultivated to yield rich harvests.

The basis of great sales production is two-way enthusiasm. One scholarly yet highly influential sales consultant declared:

> Enthusiasm that results in sales can only be aroused by an *ideal.* That ideal must be so magnetic that it seizes control of the imagination of both the prospective buyer and of the seller. The salesman must fire up his own imagination with a workable plan for activating his ideal. When he breathes life into his ideal it will sell.

At its finest, take-charge salesmanship is an ideal—a workable, productive ideal. The principle itself is an ideal. To be a take-charge salesman do this: Prospect in depth, organize, dramatize, be interesting, be helpful, crush sales hazards, be a minute-miser, make time work for you, simplify paperwork, close selling gaps by frequent call-backs, by your conduct and by your service persuade customers to work for you—to boost your stock.

By making every sales venture a command performance you can be a take-charge salesman and take charge of every sales situation. Thereby closing becomes easier and sales mount.

A steadily mounting sales record is the self-satisfying reward for achieving easier closings. It is also the richly rewarding achievement of those who are take-charge salesmen.

INDEX